The Hussite Wars: The History and Legacy of the Conflicts Between the Catholics and Protestants in Central Europe

By Charles River Editors

A contemporary depiction of Jan Hus

About Charles River Editors

Charles River Editors is a boutique digital publishing company, specializing in bringing history back to life with educational and engaging books on a wide range of topics. Keep up to date with our new and free offerings with this 5 second sign up on our weekly mailing list, and visit Our Kindle Author Page to see other recently published Kindle titles.

We make these books for you and always want to know our readers' opinions, so we encourage you to leave reviews and look forward to publishing new and exciting titles each week.

Introduction

A contemporary depiction of fighting

"Therefore, faithful Christian, seek the truth, listen to the truth, learn the truth, love the truth, tell the truth, learn the truth, defend the truth even to death." – Jan Hus

The 15th century was a pivotal era for Europe, during which it transitioned from a social and religious union under Christendom into a disparate collection of nation-states, and it was during this period that the Middle Ages came to an end and the Modern Period began.

Less than a century earlier, in the mid-14th century, the Vatican called upon England and sought financial aid in the hopes of boosting papal defenses against French forces. It was then that John Wycliffe boldly stepped forth and appealed to the John of Gaunt, urging the Duke of Lancaster and Parliament to repudiate Rome's demands and citing what he believed to be the Church's abundance in wealth. According to Wycliffe, Christ's disciples, particularly clergymen, must aspire to live modestly and shun all material pleasures. Such was the word of the Lord.

Despite the growing tensions between Wycliffe and the Catholic Church, he was invited to partake in a religious committee that aimed to find solutions for the apparent failings of the institution in 1374, but progress was slow, impeded by the corruption of the priests who readily accepted bribes and immoral incentives. Wycliffe, on the contrary, was equipped with a cast-iron will and refused to cave into temptation. His strength of character earned him the approbation of the Duke and members of Parliament. The same could not be said about his fellow clergymen.

Wycliffe's relentless criticism of the Church only continued to escalate, and eventually he was summoned to London and charged with the unforgivable crime of heresy. To the dismay of his detractors, the hearing was anything but black and white, and heated verbal exchanges soon spiraled into physical altercations. This resulted in a temporary deadlock that was broken only three months later when Pope Gregory XI published five papal bulls that unequivocally banned all of Wycliffe's teachings and found the heretic, dubbed the "master of errors," guilty of 18 counts of heresy. The end, it appeared, was nigh, but Wycliffe remained unfazed, declaring, "I profess and claim to be by the grace of God a sound...Christian and while there is breath in my body, I will speak forth and defend the law of it." Wycliffe told the archbishop at Lambeth Palace, "I am ready to defend my convictions even unto death...I have followed the Sacred Scriptures and the holy doctors."

Though branded a heretic, the renegade did not die in Christ's name, but Hus would not be so fortunate. Moreover, while Wycliffe's critics rejoiced at the news of his demise, they soon discovered that his influence was far more difficult to extinguish than they initially anticipated. In 1427, a whole 43 years after Wycliffe's passing, his corpse was exhumed by local authorities and cremated, and the ashes were dumped into the River Swift, but Wycliffe's indelible ideas had taken on a life of their own, and they would be championed by Hus. The 17th century historian Thomas Fuller poetically described the ripple effect: "Thus the brook hath conveyed his ashes into Avon; Avon into Severn; Severn into the narrow seas; and they into the main ocean. And thus the ashes of Wycliffe are the emblem of his doctrine which now is dispersed the world over."

If Wycliffe was the "Morning Star of the Reformation," Jan Hus was the Guiding Star of the movement. Hus started as a Czech priest, but he quickly became notorious for debating several Church doctrines such as the Eucharist, Church ecclesiology, and many more topics. Today, he is viewed as a predecessor of the Lutherans, but the Church viewed him as a threat, and the Catholics eventually engaged Hus' followers (known as Hussites) in several battles in the early 15th century. Hus himself was burned at the stake in 1415, but his followers fought on in a series of battles known as the Hussite Wars, and Czechoslovakia's inhabitants by and large remained Hussite afterward. About 100 years later, Martin Luther would spark the Reformation across the continents.

The Need for Reform

Christendom is the term used to express the unity of Western Christianity in the Middle Ages under two leaders: a spiritual one, the Pope, and a temporal one, the Holy Roman Emperor. The latter was created by the former in 800 when Pope Leo III placed the crown of the artificially revived Western Roman Empire upon the head of Charlemagne, but Charlemagne's great empire was divided after his death and three main successor states emerged: Germany, France and Italy. In the 10th century, the kings of Germany gained control of both northern Italy and the imperial crown, and thenceforth a struggle emerged between Pope and Emperor over the governance of the Church and of Europe. After a long and bloody struggle, the papacy emerged victorious in the twelfth century, successfully asserting its right to administer the affairs of the universal Church, particularly in regards to the appointment of bishops. Yet the papacy did more than that by advancing the right to correct and, if necessary, punish princes for violations of the Church's rights and liberties or for stubbornly failing to observe its rites and teachings. It established that emperors and kings were not equal to the pope, but subservient to him, a threat demonstrated by the Church wielding the terrible weapon of excommunication. An excommunicate meant being cut off from the Church, the sole means of salvation, and facing everlasting damnation unless the accused repented and was absolved. An excommunicated monarch lost his crown and was declared deposed, leaving him vulnerable to enemies who were only too keen to execute the sentence. Emperor Henry IV was famously excommunicated by Pope Gregory VII in 1076 and was only absolved after being made to kneel in sackcloth before the Vicar of Christ.

The Holy Roman Emperor was the temporal, if nominal, head of all of Christendom, and though he owed the crown of Germany to a college of prince-electors, he could not be emperor unless crowned by the pope in Rome. Of course, this did not mean the emperor was always compliant with the wishes of the Church; on the contrary, the relationship of pope and emperor was always a tense one, but in an open conflict the emperor would always have to come hat in hand to Rome, for its bishop possessed the power to deprive him of the crown.

Another mighty weapon used by the Church was the power to declare a crusade. Pope Urban II first preached a crusade against the Saracens in 1095 to assist the beleaguered Byzantine Empire and to unite a fractious Europe. This ability to wield military power enormously enhanced the papacy's prestige and moral authority, which reached its height during the reign of Innocent III (d. 1216), generally regarded to have been the most powerful man in Europe.

Despite holding extraordinary power, this papal empire was fundamentally fragile. It depended upon a commitment to wealth and power that a number of Christians pointed out was fundamentally inimical to the principles of the gospel of Jesus. The use of brute force to maintain its power, especially when it called the French into Italy against Sicily in the 13th century, rankled with many Christians, and widespread protest movements broke out after the 12th century. Some, like the Friars Minor of Francis of Assisi, preached poverty and service within the Catholic Church, but others such as the Cathars in southern Europe broke entirely from its dogmas and discipline. The Church responded with vigour to the latter, establishing the inquisition and targeting crusades at them, and even regarding the former with suspicion.

The papacy was challenged by the secular powers as well. The kings of France in particular began to resist its exercise of temporal power, and when Pope Boniface VIII declared that 'it is necessary for salvation that every human creature be subject to the Roman Pontiff'[1] King Philip IV had him arrested in 1303. He was rescued but died from the physical abuse inflicted upon him, and although the savagery of the event outraged Europe the statement had been made: the papal empire was at an end. In 1305 a French bishop wad elected pope and as Clement V set up court at Avignon it became evident that the pope had become a chaplain of the King of France. The period of Avignon pontiffs became known as the Babylonian captivity of the Church.

Worse humiliations were to come. Pope Gregory XI returned to Rome in 1378, but he died soon after and the refusal of his successor, Urban VI, to go back to Avignon triggered a schism in the Western Church. For the next 39 years, Christendom was divided in its allegiances between a pope in Rome and a pope in Avignon, and for a time, there was even a third pope established at Pisa. Thus, as the 15th century dawned, the Catholic Church and the papacy had reached its lowest ebb. Christendom was divided, with rival popes hurling anathemas at each other and no obvious mechanism to restore unity. The secular states filled the vacuum vacated by the Church, and a strong reform movement advocated either a return to evangelical values within the structures of the Church or a complete radicalization of dogma and discipline. The medieval empire of Christendom was collapsing, and it was by no means clear what would replace it.

Jan Hus and the Council of Constance

Like most figures born several centuries ago, concrete details about Jan Hus' life, particularly his childhood and formative years, remain hazy, and even the year of his birth remains a matter of dispute. Consensus has it that Jan of Husinecz, later shortened to "Jan Hus," was born on the 6th of July between the years of 1369 and 1373, an estimation derived from his ordination in 1401. His place of birth, as suggested by his name, was Husinecz, or "Goose-town" in English, not far from the village of Prachatice in Southern Bohemia (what is now the Czech Republic). Others have also theorized that he was born not in Husinecz, but in a village of a similar name, Husinec, which lay just a few miles away from the town of Klecany in Prague.

Even less is known about Hus' family, including their names, but chroniclers who sifted through the journals and manuscripts composed by Hus as an adult have created a narrative of sorts. What is clear is that Hus came from a poverty-stricken, but pious farming family - Hus

---

[1] Boniface VIII (1302) *Unam Sanctam*, Papal Encyclicals Online
    https://www.papalencyclicals.net/Bon08/B8unam.htm.

himself wrote that his mother was an extremely devout Christian who fully expected her children to put God above all else. It was his mother who taught him how to pray and read to him select passages from the Bohemian Bible night after night, and she instilled her children with priestly ambitions. Based on Hus' limited descriptions of his mother, he seemd to be quite close to her. She was soft-spoken, generous, and most of all, attentive, escorting her children to and from the Latin school in Prachatice, rain or shine.

Not surprisingly, the living conditions and quality of life that young Hus endured left much to be desired. Hus and his family lived in a cramped wooden cottage with a poorly thatched roof that required regular maintenance, and it amply reflected their peasant class. Their home would have been sparsely furnished, and its walls constructed out of wattle and daub, which was a latticework of sticks and twigs stiffened with a blend of straw, mud, and manure. Due to the lack of furniture, which was considered a luxury at the time, the family most likely slept and ate on the hard dirt floor. The filthy floor would have also been matted with the feces of the family's horses, sheep, and other pets, which were rounded up and brought into the cottage at night to guard them from thieves and ravenous beasts.

Hus and his siblings were trained in the agricultural arts from an early age. He started out by helping his mother sprinkle seeds along their small plot of farmland and lugging little baskets of harvested corn, potatoes, and other produce into their cottage. The chores assigned to him, as well as the level of his exertion, was proportional to his age and physical strength. By his teenage years, he was plowing the fields, tending to large batches of crops, and chopping wood for the winter.

Hus' time at the Latin school in Prachatice (which in some accounts is a schoolhouse attached to the local church) was both enriched and tainted by numerous firsts. For instance, it was the first time he took part in a choir, and school was where he stumbled upon his love for singing. He was also introduced to the controversial festival known as the "Feast of Fools." For that event, a "Boy Bishop," usually a choir boy between the ages of 7 and 12, was crowned. In England, the Boy Bishop, essentially elected to parody the actual bishop, was appointed on the 6th of December (the feast day of St. Nicholas), a mock tenure that was lifted on the 28th of December, otherwise known as the Day of Holy Innocents. In Bohemia, however, which most likely took a page from France, the festival kicked off on New Year's Day. Once elected, the Boy Bishop was accoutered in full bishop regalia, complete with crozier, a hooked ceremonial staff, and miter, the elaborately ornamented "fish-like" headdresses worn by bishops. The false bishop was also given a personal retinue of "priests" composed of randomly selected boys around his age. Together, the Boy Bishop and his entourage paraded around town, doling out blessings and performing other sacramental rituals (excluding Mass), more often than not speaking complete gibberish. Adults were expected to swap roles, too, so laymen, cooks, and gardeners took charge of the parish offices and their local choirs. Priests and other high-ranking members of the Church, in turn, donned the rags worn by the help, and they had to complete menial duties.

The following passage is a short, but concise description of the feast provided by a disgruntled attendee in a 15th century letter: "Priests and clerks may be seen wearing masks and monstrous visages at the hours of office. They dance in the choir dressed as women, panders, or minstrels. They sing wanton songs. They eat black puddings at the horn of the altar while the celebrant is saying Mass. They play at dice...They cense [sic] with stinking smoke from the soles of old shoes. They run and leap through the church, without a blush at their own shame. Finally, they drive about the town...in shabby traps and carts; and rouse the laughter of their fellows and bystanders in infamous performances, with indecent gestures and verses scurrilous and unchaste!"

To most, the feast was harmless fun, but Hus, on the other hand, was not at all impressed by the bright colors, endless carousing, and cross-dressing revelry. He found it to be a bizarre and reprehensible tradition, but the young Bible-hugger, perhaps intimidated by the idea of going against the grain at such an early age, kept mum and played along. One of Hus' later journal entries reveals his true stance on the practice, as well as his remorse for his participation in these depraved feasts: "What manifest outrage they perpetrate in the church by wearing masks. In my youthfulness, I also was once to my shame a masquerader!...Having [been] designated a cleric, dressed in monstrous attire, as bishop, they cause him to sit backwards on an ass with his face turned towards the tail. Then, they take him into the church to Mass. They carry a plate of broth in front of him, and a jug or can of beer, and he eats in the church. I saw how the ass incenses the altars and, raising one leg, calls out in a loud voice, 'Boo!', and the priests carry before him large torches instead of candles. He rides from one altar to another altar, incensing as he goes. And I observed how the priests turned their fur-lined vestments inside out and danced in the church...All the people watch this and laugh, thinking that all of this is holy and proper, since it appears in their rubric and in their statutes. Nice statutes, alright! What undisciplined abomination!...When I was still young, both in years and in reason, I am ashamed to say that I also adhered to this crazy rubric. But when the Lord God helped me understand the Scriptures, I eliminated such notions and the statutes of delusion from my weak intellect."

Hus' reluctance to immerse himself in the annual, nationally celebrated feast was only one example of his piety, which was remarkably robust for a kid his age. According to one account, the God-fearing young man took his devotion to an entirely new level. Hus, as the story goes, was curled up by the hearth one winter evening with the tattered pages of his precious St. Lawrence biography illuminated by the crackling fire. In early summer of 258 CE, Valerian, the pagan emperor of Rome, sentenced all Christian priests, bishops, and deacons (including Lawrence) to be burned at the stake. Before their inescapable executions, the condemned were ordered to empty the treasuries of their churches and surrender all their possessions to the prefect of Rome. With a twinkle in his eye, Hus read about how Lawrence was granted the three days he requested to collect his belongings, tidy up the church, and tie up other loose ends. Indeed, this was precisely what he did, but rather than set aside his personal valuables and holdings, as he was instructed, he sold them all and distributed the profits, as well as the church's funds, to the destitute.

In 1390, Hus enrolled at the Charles University of Prague, where he chose to study in the department of Arts, Philosophy, and Theology. Naturally, penury followed him into his university years, so he resided in a student boarding house, and apart from rent, he coughed up a *heller* (coin valued at 1/100 of a *koruna*) to the proprietor for a beer to accompany his small meals. Hus also secured a job as a *famulus* (a kind of servant) to Stephen of Kolin, his professor of theology, provost (senior academic administrator) of the Carolinum dormitory, and rector of the local Bethlehem Chapel. For that, Hus received a modest salary.

Hus was awarded his Bachelor of Arts degree in the autumn of 1393, placing sixth in a class of 22. John of Myto, another one of Hus' professors, was listed as the master of the ceremony. For his commencement speech, the host quoted the philosopher Aristotle, discussing how one must suffer and emerge from adversity in order to achieve a gratifying sense of well-being. When Hus was summoned to accept his diploma, he was commended by Myto for his diligence and the hard work he put forth for his degree. Hus, Myto insisted, was a "student [who] strove for mental health and intelligence at the cost of his [own] physical health," and he concluded his speech with a neat goose-related pun. A year later, Hus was awarded his Bachelor of Arts degree in Divinity, and in the autumn of 1396, Hus was presented his Master's degree in Divinity, this time placing 10th in his class of 16.

Contrary to popular belief, as religious and ostensibly conservative as the young man was, he was not the morally high-strung and uptight individual many might imagine he was. While he was indeed an attentive and above-average student, he also very much enjoyed carousing with his friends. Hus himself admitted "to have been overly fond of elegant clothes and gambling," among other "roistering escapades."

Hus attended Sunday service without fail, but rather than fork over what little he had to the offertory, he dedicated his funds to booze and other activities with his friends. He rubbed shoulders with moneyed masters, professors, and friends, gorging on delicious meals on their dimes and strutting about in borrowed silk robes whenever he was afforded the opportunity. He began to neglect his Bible, instead playing round after round of chess and other time-wasting tabletop games. The charismatic college student also possessed an astoundingly bizarre sense of humor, having been particularly fond of dirty jokes, smutty double entendres, and tasteless pranks, and Hus often found himself ensnarled in tussles, mostly instigated by his chess opponents and the targets of his practical jokes. Even more surprising, the young man avoided not only asceticism, but celibacy, and frequently spent the evening with the wanton women who snuck into the all-male boarding houses. Those who knew him in his later life would have been stunned to discover that young Hus cared quite deeply about his external appearance and his artificial social status, as he was finally granted the prestige he had been yearning for all his life.

Hus explained in his diary, "Therefore, I confess my wicked desire that when I was a schoolboy, I thought about soon becoming a priest in order to have a good livelihood, and robes and [sic] to have the respect of the people."

This was the immodest lifestyle Hus led for the first three years of his university career. His transition to the virtuous, scrupulous Hus revered by Christians today was exactly that: a piecemeal process.

In 1393, just a few months after Hus received his Bachelor's degree, he wandered into a service at the Bethlehem Chapel led by one of his former professors, a Cistercian monk named Father Jan Stekna, to celebrate the Jubilee. Hus' eyes were glued to the captivating monk throughout the entirety of the sermon, and he watched with rapt attention as Stekna dissected the concept and discussed the importance of spiritual indulgences by citing the luxurious lives of the residents of the castle Vysehrad, located just south of Prague's town square. Indulgences, Stekna explained, were symbolic of the debts one owed to the Lord for their sins; in other words, by paying off one's debts, one shows that they are truly repentant, and only then would they be granted forgiveness. Stekna also expounded on the shelf life of these indulgence certificates and detailed why it was necessary to purchase these certificates regularly. The phenomenon was mutually beneficial to both the Church and the purchaser of these certificates, said Stekna, for it cleansed the transgressor of their sins and helped their local church stay afloat.

Hus, perhaps subconsciously affected by guilt over his libertine behavior, was so moved by Stekna's sermon that he traveled to Vysehrad, where Stekna was based. Once there, he emptied his purse and presented to the monk his last four *groschen* in exchange for an indulgence certificate, hoping to wash away some of the sins he had accumulated in recent years. He could only appease his grumbling gut with small wedges of dry, flavorless bread in the days or weeks that followed, but to Hus, it was well worth it. Thomas A. Fudge, author of *Jan Hus: Religious Reform and Social Revolution in Bohemia*, explained, "[Hus,] a firm believer in the merits of the indulgence...seemed prepared to be penniless and live a life of utter poverty so long as he possessed the assurance of the forgiveness of sins."

It seemed Hus' religious zeal was making its swift return, and he vowed to retire his "deviant" lifestyle and devote his life to the path of righteousness. Little did he know that he would soon chance upon a book that would forever reshape not only his views on the ethics of indulgences, but the Church itself.

In 1398, Hus was appointed examiner, lecturer at the Faculty of Arts, and a professor of theology at his alma mater, which was a requisite for his master's degree. A total of 23 students were placed under his charge, and it was his goal to secure the post of master at Charles University, but his progress was thwarted by the rambling queue of qualified professionals vying for the same position. At the time, the university was home to 500 bachelor of arts holders, about 200 doctors, and 30,000 eager students.

During the weekends, Hus continued to assist and sing for the choirs of the local churches. His work ethic and perseverance eventually paid off, as he was ordained as a priest in the summer of 1400. He had at long last entered the clergy, but he was not bound to any one church, so he preached at the Church of St. Michael in the Old Town and other parishes in the neighborhood. Hus was overjoyed by his ordination - not only was he now licensed to spread the gospel, he was finally granted the financial security and satisfactory standard of living he had been pining after for so long. At the same time, Hus continued to plug away at his academic career, which resulted in a promotion to dean of the philosophical department at the university in 1401.

On the 14th of March in the following year, Hus was hired as one of the resident preachers at the Bethlehem Chapel and thereupon began to refer to himself as the "rector and preacher in the Chapel of the Holy Innocents of Bethlehem in the old and great city of Prague." He wore the wordy title like a badge of honor, as he was proud to be part of such a prominent and thriving institution. Although the chapel was erected in 1391, just 11 years before his appointment, the church had become one of the largest religious establishments in all of Europe, boasting well over 3,000 members.

As thrilled as he was to now be formally attached to a parish, Hus immediately took notice of the shortcomings of his seemingly impressionable and potentially corruptible colleagues, as well as the problematic system employed by his workplace. As Hus himself later confessed, he decided against ruffling any feathers for fear of losing his newly acquired position, choosing instead to give his colleagues the benefit of the doubt. What it was that changed his mind is still debated to this day.

As previously mentioned, there was not a singular, metamorphic "conversion experience" that opened his eyes to his own infirmities and the disappointing failings of the Church. According to Hus, "When the Lord gave me knowledge of Scriptures, I discharged from my foolish mind that kind of stupid fun-making, and in time, saw the light." The majority of his biographers, however, believe that John Wycliffe played an instrumental role in steering Hus towards his ultimate path.

Wycliffe

Hus was first introduced to Wycliffe by Jerome of Prague, a close friend of his and a fellow martyr in the making, in 1402. Upon returning from his trip to England, Jerome loaned Hus a collection of Wycliffe's works, which he had painstakingly copied by hand while studying at Oxford University. Jerome proclaimed, "Young men and students who did not study the books of Wycliffe would never find the true root of knowledge." Curiously, Jerome conveniently failed to mention the reformer's troubling reputation, namely that he had been branded a blasphemous heretic by the religious authorities in England. Even more concerning, Wycliffe's devotees were being forced to disavow the heretic, and those who refused were promptly executed.

Hus was eventually apprised of Wycliffe's reputation by an unidentified friend who caught him scrutinizing the English reformer's texts. That friend attempted to coax him into chucking the dangerous literature into the Vlatva River, but Hus, who had become deeply engrossed in Wycliffe's unorthodox, but compelling ideas, would do no such thing. His admiration for the reformer was evinced in the notes he scrawled on the margins of the manuscripts, one of which read, "Dear Wycliffe, may God grant you eternal bliss...Wycliffe, you will turn many a head."

A contemporary depiction of Wycliffe's books being burned

Wycliffe, who was frustrated with the deterioration of the Church and the delinquency of its officials, had campaigned to restore order to the institution. First and foremost, he questioned the concept of transubstantiation, "the change by which the substance...of the bread and wine in the Eucharist becomes Christ's Real Presence – that is, his body and blood…The bread while becoming by virtue of Christ's words the body of Christ does not cease to be bread." He picked apart the sacrament of confession: "Private confession...was not ordered by Christ, and was not used by the apostles." He urged all Christians to forgo the Church's dubious new-age teachings, and to return to Christ. "Trust wholly in Christ," wrote Wycliffe. "Rely altogether on his sufferings. Beware of seeking to be justified in any other way than by his righteousness."

Furthermore, Wycliffe protested against the installation of two popes, as well as the papacy itself. "England belongs to no pope," Wycliffe declared in his Civil Dominion of 1376. "The pope is but a man, subject to sin, but Christ is the Lord of Lords and this kingdom is to be held directly and solely of Christ alone."

What truly caught Hus' attention was Wycliffe's scathing criticism of simony and indulgences. Wycliffe railed against the practice, writing, "The indulgences of the pope...are a manifest blasphemy, in as much as he claims a power to save men almost without limit, and not only to mitigate the penalties of those who have sinned, by granting them the aid of absolution and indulgences, that they may never come to purgatory...The friars give a color to this blasphemy, by saying that Christ is omnipotent...and that the pope is his plenary vicar on earth, and so possesses in everything the same power as Christ in his humanity."

Hus was also moved by Wycliffe's initiative, especially his decision to translate the Latin Bible into English with the help of John Purvey. The Church, inevitably, resisted the idea, and officials asserted, "By this translation, the Scriptures have become vulgar, and they are more available to lay, and even to women who can read, than they were to learned scholars, who have a high intelligence. So the pearl of the gospel is scattered and trodden underfoot by swine." Still, Wycliffe stood his ground, replying, "Englishmen learn Christ's law best in English. Moses heard God's law in his own tongue; so did Christ's apostles." This was most likely what motivated Hus to modernize the Bohemian Bible in later years.

Hus also found muses among local theologians. One of them was Konrád Waldhauser, an Australian author, preacher, and reformer who was invited to Prague in 1363 by Emperor Charles IV. Waldhauser's sermons, which stressed the importance of Scripture and censured the avarice of local priests and simony practitioners, were supposedly so popular that they attracted various sects of the Christian faith and even Jews. Waldhauser's lambasting of the Church, naturally, incited the wrath of the city's clerics, but he, too, persisted with his fiery campaign.

Soon thereafter, Waldhauser's ideas were adopted by Milic of Kromerize, also hailed as one of the fathers of the Bohemian reformation. Milic's preaching style, characterized as "entirely biblical" as opposed to "scholastic," earned him equal shares of praise and condemnation. He spotlighted the rise of the "anti-christ" and the "abomination of desolation" running rampant within the Church, but his assertion that ascetic, devout laymen were morally superior to unrighteous clergymen was what fueled most enmity towards him.

It was only after being introduced to the aforementioned reformers' ideas that Hus began his crusade against the Church. Hus honed in on Father Bernard, the leader of St. Michael's Church, whom he called "a very great enemy of the Word of God." He confronted the incumbent head of the establishment at private dinners, arguing with him about the various inconsistencies of the Church's doctrine. When Hus realized that their heated exchanges were bearing no fruit, he made the Church's backwards canons the subject of his sermons.

A contemporary depiction of Hus preaching

Although Hus refrained from singling Bernard out in his sermons, the church leader was still livid about the tendentious preacher's apparent mission to divide the already crumbling congregation. Bernard stormed into Hus' living quarters and vehemently demanded that he put an end to his "misguided" tirades at once. Perhaps fearing the forfeiture of his newly-acquired post, Hus grudgingly agreed to water down his criticisms for the time being.

Although Hus undoubtedly placed Wycliffe on a pedestal, he did not share all of the reformer's beliefs. Joseph Kalmer and Paul Roubiczek, authors of *Warrior of God: The Life and Death of John Hus,* note that Hus "did not fiercely attack the adoration of saints, nor the medieval church service...he only fought against the abuses within the church." He was also not opposed to the idea of transubstantiation; instead, he urged the Church to administer to all laypersons full communion. At the time, laypersons were only allowed to consume the body of Christ, while the blood of Christ was reserved for priests.

Not surprisingly, Hus initially had no intentions of creating a new sect. Trevor O'Reggio, author of *John Huss and the Origins of the Protestant Reformation* explained, "Hus was not calling for any new doctrine, but for what he believed was a restoration of pure Christianity as taught in the Bible. Although at first, theological and devotional, the Bohemian reformation swiftly turned into a social revolution. As Hus began to see more clearly the errors of the church, the gap between the Bohemian reformers and the establishment became so wide that their views became irreconcilable."

Church leaders were unquestionably fearful of Hus' increasing influence within the community, and rightfully so. Though he was barely 30, he had access to tens of thousands of pliable minds, a tremendous congregation that most in his position could only dream of in Europe. Throughout the 12 years of Hus' tenure at Bethlehem Chapel, he headlined over 3,500 sermons (twice a day every Sunday), and that doesn't count the services he held in neighboring churches. Christians from all walks of life, ranging from lowly peasants and artisans to nobility (including Queen Sophia of Bavaria, the consort of King Wenceslaus IV) poured into the chapel unfailingly every week, anxious to hear the electrifying sermons of the young priest.

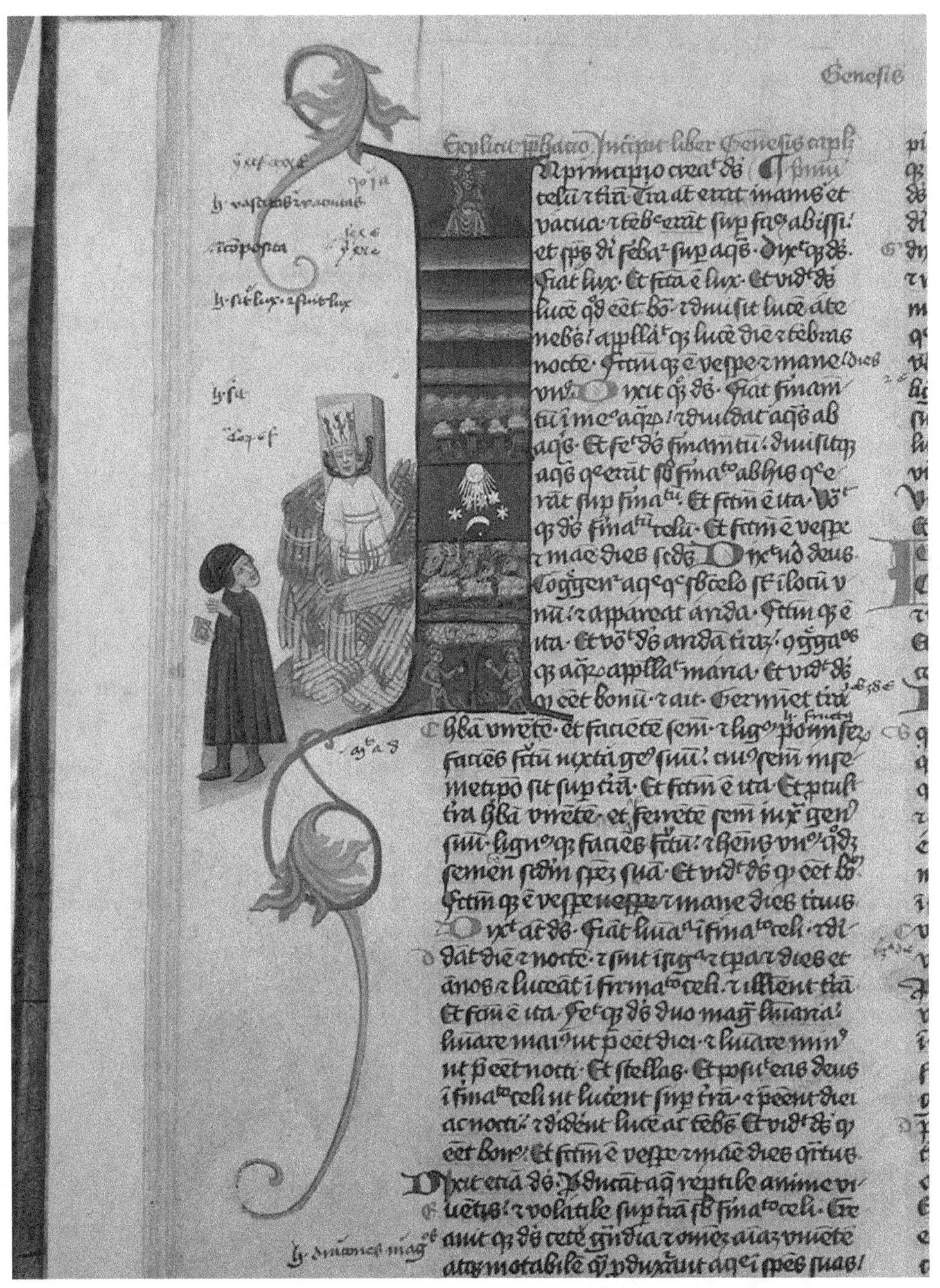

The Martinická Bible's representation of Hus, the oldest known surviving depiction of him

Unwilling to squander the prodigious platform that he had been gifted, Hus quickly revived his campaign against the corruptions of the Church. The sanctity of rectitude and repentance, Hus declared, had been sullied, as sinners were committing sins everywhere, pursuing extramarital affairs and engaging in all forms of debauchery. They no longer felt the need to honor the laws laid down by Scripture, for they were now protected by a sheet of paper that allegedly cleansed them of all wrongdoing. One could even purchase indulgences on behalf of their family and friends, deceased or otherwise, a concept that made no sense to traditionalists such as Hus.

Simony aside, Hus preached against the wave of fake miracles that had taken Europe by storm. He took issue with the false relics displayed by the greedy proprietors of churches near and far, insisting that they were only interested in the donations the relics attracted. One church, for example, was caught when their relic, purportedly a brain fragment belonging to St. Peter, was found to be nothing more than a hunk of pumice stone. John Calvin would later remark, "If all the relics were brought together in one place, it would be made manifest that every apostle has more than four bodies, and every saint two or three."

Unwanted foreign intervention was yet another lesser-mentioned facet of the Bohemian reformers' opposition towards the Church. Matthew Spinka and Frantisek M. Bartos, who wrote Hus' biography on *Encyclopedia Britannica*, elaborated on this: "At this time, the University of Prague was undergoing a period of struggle against foreign, chiefly German, influence as well as an intense rivalry between, on the one hand, German masters who upheld nominalism and were regarded as enemies of church reform, and on the other, the strongly nationalistic Czech masters, who were inclined to realist philosophy." A relevant excerpt from one of Hus' sermons read, "The Czechs in this part are more wretched than dogs or snakes, for a dog defends the couch on which he lies, and if another dog tries to drive him away, he fights with him. A snake does the same. But we let the Germans oppress us and occupy all the offices, without complaint."

The reformers' conflict with the Catholic Church ran much deeper than disagreements regarding indulgences and false relics. The Church controlled roughly half of Bohemian territory, ownership that invited decades of dormant resentment from the land's disgruntled residents. Local low-earning priests such as Hus were especially aggrieved at the seemingly untouchable affluence and irreproachable status of the Church, and peasants also complained about the hefty land taxes the Church imposed upon them. Thus, there was plenty of promise for the budding reformation movement in Bohemia.

In October 1402, Hus was appointed rector of Charles University, but his promotion was short-lived. By the spring of 1403, the Wycliffe backlash, which initially began as an incipient trend, had reached a frenzied pitch, and when Hus was outed as one of Wycliffe's most vocal adherents, he was immediately sacked and replaced with a German master named Walter Harrasser. On May 28, 1403, Harrasser published an edict that prohibited the discussion of 24 Wycliffian articles, echoing the ban issued by the English officials at the Blackfriars Synod back in May 1382. Not long after, Johann Hubner added another 21 articles to the list and labeled all 45 of these articles "heretical." Topping the list was the condemnation of transubstantiation.

Nonetheless, Hus remained undeterred. Just a few months later, he translated one of Wycliffe's treatises, *Trialogus*, into the Bohemian language and disseminated the forbidden literature to his congregation.

Eventually, the archbishopric protection granted to Hus wore off, and it was discontinued by Pope Innocent VII himself. On June 24, 1405, Zajic received orders from the pope to unequivocally repudiate Wycliffism. Left with no choice but to assent to the higher power, Zajic issued a synodal decree that banned all Wycliffian texts and prevented reformers such as Hus from taking the immoral priests to task.

Pope Innocent VII

Hus lamented the loss of his powerful ally, but he remained undaunted. In 1406, a pair of Bohemian students returned from their trip to England, bringing with them a new Wycliffian manuscript secured by the official seal of the University of Oxford. The following morning, Hus defied the anti-Wycliffe decrees once more when he recited the manuscript in full from his pulpit at the Bethlehem Chapel. Priests observing from afar erupted in a flurry of whispers, and it would not be long before Pope Innocent VII's successor, Pope Gregory XII, learned of Hus' insubordination. Furious, the pope authored another letter addressed to Archbishop Zajic, berating him for his inability to rein in the remaining Wycliffe supporters and warning him about King Wenceslaus IV's excessive leniency towards the reformers. Not wanting to provoke the pope any further, the king proposed that Wycliffe's work be submitted to the archdiocesan chancery for a more in-depth analysis, followed by revisions. Sensing the potential loss of another valuable ally, Hus complied - after all, he also disagreed with some of Wycliffe's ideas. This was a wise move, as it kept the king in his corner for some time, a situation made all the more vital by the fact he was losing allies.

Pope Gregory XII

A late 14th century depiction of King Wenceslaus IV from the Wenceslas Bible

Hus was most disillusioned by Archbishop Zajic, who Hus felt had demonstrated a complete change of heart in less than five years. In 1407, the archbishop targeted Palec and Stanislav, Hus' closest companions, and charged them with heresy, sentencing them for an immediate examination at the Roman Curia. To Hus' dismay, Palec and Stanislav were propagandized, so much so that they emerged at the forefront of the anti-reform movement and severed all ties with Hus. In fact, Palec, who once clung to the reformer, became so antipathetic to the nonconformist's ideas that he actively campaigned to have Hus condemned as a heretic.

Throughout the entire ordeal, Hus became convinced that the loss of his allies was no more than a test put forth by God, so he regrouped and kept pushing on, determined to bring his true beliefs to the masses. An unnamed author, as documented by O'Reggio, explained the significance of the controversial, but flourishing movement: "Religious conflict, reinforced by social factors, broke out and as the socially and religiously discontented in Bohemia were almost exclusively Czechs, it gained an irresistible momentum. The part played by national feeling made this revolt unique. For the first time in modern history, a united nation was to rise in arms. It was fighting for its faith, but national feeling, particularly strong for social reasons, was also engaged. For the first time, the overwhelming and fateful strength of national feeling was revealed. John Hus [personified] the fusion of these three compelling forces."

In 1408, as the tensions brought about by the Western Schism continued to escalate, King Wenceslaus IV published a decree that called upon all Bohemian residents to take a strict stance of neutrality when it came to the two rival popes, Gregory XII and Benedict XIII. The Czech members of Charles University, Hus included, abided by the order with no hesitation, but Archbishop Zajic and the German university professors protested against the edict and resolutely sided with Pope Gregory, chiefly due to his fierce opposition towards the reformists and his support of the Germans. Insulted by their insolence, King Wenceslaus IV retaliated by restructuring the university charter on January 18, 1409 via the Decree of Kutna Hora. Before the decree, staff members from each nation (Bohemians, Bavarians, Saxons, and Poles) were each allowed one single vote apiece, but the new decree granted three votes to the Bohemians and only one vote to the rest of the nations, which rendered the system pointless. As a result, irate German students, professors, and masters left the university in droves, which had a clear impact on the institution's directory since Germans previously made up approximately 70% of the university body. The Decree of Kutna Hora was specially tailored to suit the needs of the reformer, and with the ball now permanently in the court of the Bohemians, resistance against the movement would be vastly reduced. More importantly, Hus was now entitled to preach whatever he pleased on the university grounds.

On June 26, 1409, the Council of Cardinals (otherwise known as the "Council of Pisa") took place. In a convoluted and ultimately failed bid to depose the rival popes and end the Western Schism, the attendees of the conference elected Pietro Cardinal Philarghi, also known as Antipope Alexander V, into the office. Hus and his followers, as instructed by King Wenceslaus IV, agreed to serve under the authority of the antipope with little fuss. The archbishop, much of the senior clergy, and what was left of the Germans remained faithful to Gregory behind closed doors.

Antipope Alexander V

As a reward for his compliance, Hus was reinstated as the rector of the university on October 17, 1409. This reacquired position provided him with eminence amongst his peers, and he was given precedence over academic matters and other general affairs. Many now consider his appointment as university rector to be the pinnacle of his overall career, a time when his once-stellar reputation, though somewhat blemished, was still intact.

Archbishop Zajic viewed Hus' allegiance to the antipope as yet another act of betrayal, but Zajic could not afford to antagonize the king, taking note of his isolation given the absence of his German comrades. As such, the archbishop outwardly pledged his allegiance to Antipope Alexander V, but not without a trick up his sleeve. In the hopes of turning the situation around, Zajic supposedly extended to the antipope a series of substantial bribes, and in return he was granted a number of favors.

Zajic then filed an official statement of protest against Wycliffe and his followers, accusing them of inciting "ecclesiastical disturbances," and Antipope Alexander V, now in Zajic's camp, authorized a papal bull on December 20, 1409 that vested the archbishop and other senior clergy with the power to prosecute Wycliffe devotees, thereby nullifying the protection and perks granted to Hus by the Decree of Kutna Hora. The bull also reiterated the ban on all reformative Wycliffe material and preaching in public and private places of worship alike, "even those which had privileges granted by the Apostolic See," for good measure.

Once the bull came into effect, the archbishop ordered everyone in the kingdom to surrender all Wycliffe related manuscripts to the cardinal's representative. Those who neglected to act accordingly within six days were swiftly excommunicated, no questions asked. Zajic's men then built a blazing bonfire and began feeding wagons upon wagons of literature, including *Trialogus* (which Hus had translated), *Dialogus,* and *De Eucharista,* to the flames as the haunting toll of their bells spilled across the open space. Hus beseeched the antipope to reconsider, but Alexander V's ss decision was final.

Still undaunted, the indefatigable Hus refused to change his sermons at Bethlehem Chapel. What's more, in another show of defiance, the relentless reformer taught and led his congregation in belting out new, unapproved worship songs (some possibly composed by Hus himself) during services. Frantisek Palacky, a renowned 19th century Czech historian, detailed the efficacy and potency of Hus' style of preaching: "The sermons preached during many years by this man in the Bethlehem Chapel of...Prague were among the most important events of his time. Less coarse in his sermons than Waldhauser, less exaggerated in his views than Milic, he did not affect his hearers so powerfully as his predecessors, and yet his success was far more lasting. He appealed especially to the common sense of his hearers, aroused their interest, taught and convinced them, and yet he was not lacking in impressiveness. Several attributes raised him far above his colleagues and contemporaries. Among these were keenness and clearness of his mind, the tact with which he penetrated to the very heart of a question, the ease with which he knew how to develop it [sic] before the eyes of all, the wide reading, especially in the Holy Scriptures, and the firmness and logic with which he proved a whole system of principles…To all this, we may add the deep earnestness of his character, his devout spirit, a personal conduct in which even his enemies could find nothing to blame, a burning zeal for the moral elevation of the people, as well as the reformation of the ecclesiastical conditions of his time...which looked upon the martyr's crown as the highest goal of human life."

By this stage, Hus was no stranger to being in the crosshairs of authorities, but whereas many in his shoes might've chosen to abort their endeavors, the tireless reformer's audacity only grew. In August 1408, just a few months prior to the implementation of the Kutna Hora Decree, local clerics accused Hus of sacrilegious speech. The preacher, the clerics claimed, professed to know the perennial location of Wycliffe's soul, but the accused denied that he had ever made such a claim, offering an explanation which suggested that the predestination of man is indeterminable. The accusations were reasonably minor, and the allegations against him were quickly put aside, but his accusers would not forget the imputation. They preserved the records, gradually assembling an airtight case against him.

In the spring of 1409, Hus was summoned again, this time due to charges foisted upon him by Master Marik Rvacka. A board of judges marshaled by Rvacka and his associates interrogated him for the anti-Catholic rhetoric in his treatises, referencing the preacher's works dating from 1399-1409. Hus, as ordered by his inquisitors, could only answer "yes" or "no," a strategic directive that complicated his defense. Historians consider this the Church's first official attempt to declare him a heretic. They were particularly outraged by Hus' negative stance on Donatism, defined by Father Matthew Flatley of *The Catholic Missourian* as "[a system that suggests] that Christian clergy must be faultless in order for their ministry to be effective and their prayers and sacraments to be valid." Fortunately for Hus, the evidence against him was deemed insufficient, and the matter was put to rest.

Hus could only stay one step ahead of his adversaries for so long, and when he staunchly refused to relinquish his Wycliffe texts by the deadline, incontrovertibly defying the papal bull, he was accused of "opposing the Catholic faith," branded a heretic and the wretched leader of Bohemian Wycliffism, and excommunicated.

Hus and his followers – the first generation of "Hussites" – set out to cause havoc, and Hus fanned the flames from his pulpit, denouncing both the archbishop and the antipope to roaring applause. Hus' supporters at the university displayed their solidarity by leading and partaking in protests, flaunting their disapprobation of Zajic and Antipope Alexander V and unabashedly championing Wycliffe and Hus. Hus' most faithful companion, the same Jerome of Prague who acquainted him with Wycliffe in the first place, spearheaded many of these rallies. The demonstrators chanted as they marched around their circuits:

"Zbinek, Bishop A, B, C,

Burnt the books, but ne'er knew he,

What was in them written!"

When Hus' followers caught wind of the archbishopric sermon against him on July 22, 1410, a mob took to the streets with blades and clubs in hand. According to one chronicler, in St. Stephen's Church, "six men with drawn swords tried to slay a blaspheming preacher." Another group broke away, stormed into a nearby cathedral, and chased away 40 priests. The clerics were so frightened by the violent backlash that they dared not to honor the excommunication, though the order remained in effect.

For reasons that remain unclear, the relationship between Hus and King Wenceslaus IV remained whole. Having had enough, the king and his queen consort endeavored to bring about a cessation of the hostilities, and eventually he succeeded in persuading Zajic to drop the heresy charges and lift the excommunication order on Hus. Though the archbishop agreed, he did little to mask his reluctance, and even less to fulfill his promises.

The Hussites pounced on the opportunity to groom the new antipope, Baldassare Cardinal Cossa (John XXIII), after he was elected in the wake of the untimely death of Alexander V roughly two months before the riots. Hus and his devotees appeared before Antipope John XXIII and implored him to overturn the commission installed by his predecessor. R. Martin Pope and Herbert B. Workman of the *Online Library of Liberty* break down the Hussites' defense in the following passage: "They had obtained, they pleaded, the books of Wycliffe 'at great trouble and cost.' Only a fool 'would condemn to be burnt treatises, logical, philosophical, mathematical, moral, which contain many noble truths, but no errors. By the same reasoning we must burn the books of Aristotle, the commentaries of Averrhoes, or the works of Origen [sic].' They further protested against the charge that Bohemia was full of heretics, quoting against Zajic his own declaration. Alexander's bull, they concluded, was obtained by fraud and forgery."

Antipope John XXIII

Sometime in the early months of 1411, King Wenceslaus IV finally managed to push the Hussites and the archbishop's camp one step closer to reconciliation by convincing both parties to agree to a truce. However, this period of peace proved fleeting, and in the autumn of that same year, Antipope John XXIII launched a vigorous campaign against King Ladislaus of Naples, a stalwart defender of Pope Gregory XII and the Roman Catholic Church. To finance this crusade, the antipope issued a papal bull in March of 1412 that guaranteed forgiveness via indulgence purchases to all those who contributed to the cause.

Disregarding the objections of King Wenceslaus IV, Hus took to his pulpit and delivered a polemic against the antipope's bull, a derisive speech entitled "Questions of Master Jan Hus On the Subject of Indulgences." In addition to his usual criticism of indulgences, Hus criticized the popes for not just encouraging war, but actually waging it.

The unswervingly dedicated Hussites then took matters into their own hands. Jerome mobilized another band of student protesters, who were tasked with seizing all the indulgence certificates they could get their hands on and setting them ablaze. Some protesters took it one step further by hurling a copy of the papal bull into the flames.

Their blatant irreverence towards the sacred document was later used against both Hus and Jerome. A letter from the infuriated Town Council read, "Master Jerome, we are astonished at your lighting up a fire, in which you run the risk of being burned yourself!" Many of Jerome's loved ones begged him to put a stop to the protests and abandon his allegiance towards Hus, but like his idol, his iron will was unshakable. He served nobly as a mouthpiece for Hus, preaching both verbally and by quill against clerical corruption, indulgences, simony, and iconodulism (the veneration of religious images and icons). Jerome thundered, "They who cease to preach [for Hus and genuine Scripture] will be reputed traitors in the day of judgment."

The Hussites' crusade against indulgences was momentous in more ways than one, for this, as O'Reggio explains, "marked the beginning of the loss of support from the king." On July 10, 1412, three layman Hus devotees – Martin Kridelko, Jan Hudec of Slany, and Stasek Polak – carried their anti-indulgence protests into a string of local churches, including the St. James Church, the T'yn Church, and the St. Vitus, Wenceslaus, and Aldabert Cathedral in Prague Castle. They caused such a commotion with their thunderous chants and unabating heckling that they were dragged into custody and tossed behind bars on the very same day. Not one to desert his disciples, Hus marched into city hall, accompanied by a dizzying cortege of about 2,000 students and university masters, and demanded their release. "Do not punish them for my actions," Hus appealed to the magistrates. "It was I, and I alone, who initiated this crusade." Hus' pleas fell on deaf ears, and the very next day, all three were beheaded at the execution grounds of the custom house.

According to a contemporary chronicler, a group of Hussites stealthily retrieved the corpses of the slain three, and prepared for them an impromptu procession "with great boldness." The procession, which began at the town square and concluded in Bethlehem Chapel, was accompanied by the cavalcade's somber intonation of the phrase "Isti sunt sancti." Following the procession, the bodies were swaddled in lace-white linen at the hands of female Hussites, and the cocooned corpses were buried in the chapel graveyard the next day, with Hus performing martyrial rites rather than the traditional funeral rites. Hus called the slain trio "more valuable than their weight in gold...I would not surrender their bodies for all the money in the world." Kridelko, Hudec, and Polak are now remembered as the first martyrs of the Hussite movement.

Archbishop Albik, who succeeded Zajic following his death in September 1411, did his utmost to talk Hus into discontinuing the movement, but the reformer had reached the point of no return. Likewise, the exasperated King Wenceslaus IV attempted to restore harmony between the opposing parties one last time, but this was again futile, and with that, he stopped trying.

Not long after the execution of the Hussite trio, Michael de Causis, the resident prosecutor of the papal curia, lodged a comprehensive complaint – carefully curated from the interactions between Hus and the Church over the years – on behalf of the Prague clergy. Antipope John XXIII gave his approval, entrusting the cardinal's office with proceeding against Hus and the Hussites.

Cardinal Peter degli Stephaneschi, acting accordingly, issued an arrest warrant of sorts for the reformer. Hus, as dictated by the edict, was to be arrested and made to appear before the Curia, and the Bethlehem Chapel was to be shuttered and razed to the ground, effective immediately. If Hus neglected to present himself, the Curia was entitled to impose even stricter restrictions upon him. Not only would the reformer be categorically excommunicated a second time, his city of residence would be placed under interdict, meaning that the city's residents were prohibited from receiving sacramental rites and ecclesiastical privileges.

Hus chose not to appear before the Curia, which he believed to be a surefire death sentence, but he was also unwilling to deprive the civilians of their ecclesiastical entitlements and sanctitude, so he fled to a remote area in the outskirts of the city and went into hiding. The charges against Hus and his status as a fugitive proved to be enough for King Wenceslaus IV to wash his hands of Hus completely.

When exactly Hus went into hiding is unknown, but most chroniclers estimate it to be sometime in early December 1412. It is thought that he camped out in southern Bohemia until the spring of 1414. He originally resided in one of the spare rooms of the Gothic Kozi Hradek Castle in the Tabor district before moving on to the small town of Sezimovo Usti, situated roughly 4.3 miles west of the previous castle. He remained in Sezimovo Usti for approximately a year or so, then moved once more in mid-July 1414, relocating to Krakovec Castle in West Prague. He reportedly stayed there until October.

To keep himself busy while on the run, Hus authored at least 15 books and treatises. In the Kozi Hradek Castle, the reformer completed *Expositions of the Faith*, an exhaustive commentary on classic Catholic prayers and laws that included sections on the Ten Commandments, the Lord's Prayer, and the Apostles' Creed.

Another one of his earlier titles was *De Sex Erroribus, (Six Heresies of the Church)* which was essentially a succinct summary of Hus' core beliefs and teachings. The first heresy, according to the reformer, pertained to creation. Hus slammed Church leaders for the claim that they are able to repeatedly "recreate Christ," whereas Mary could only do so once.

The second heresy pertained to what he considered the Catholic Church's excessive veneration of Mary, the saints, and the pope. In the same breath, the reformer denounced the concept of papal infallibility, and he urged Christians to hold the pope accountable for injustices, such as papal bulls that failed to align with Scripture. The Scripture, he reminded readers, would always and forever hold supremacy over mortal church leaders and clerics.

The third heresy involved the forgiveness of sins through the sale of indulgences. Only God had the power to purify one of their sins, so the purchasing of these certificates was as contradictory to Scripture as it was fruitless. Priests, Hus asserted, should instead direct their efforts towards teaching laymen how to properly seek repentance. Hus wrote, "He should say, 'Dear brother, as you repent your sins and ask the merciful Savior to forgive them, your sins are forgiven.'"

The fourth heresy called into question the imperfect nature of priests. While placing one's trust in the words of priests was a given, Hus encouraged his readers to trust their instincts and to speak out if they ever felt misled by their ministry, should the situation call for it.

The fifth heresy challenged the anathema, the term for the papal curse of excommunication. Hus blasted the callousness of the irrevocable order of exclusion and deplored the absence of brotherly love.

Last, but not least, the sixth heresy concerned simony, the sale of ecclesiastical posts, roles, and benefices. In that vein, he called upon all priests and religious role models to straighten up their acts, citing their predilection for bribes, embezzlement, alcohol abuse, and lack of asceticism, among other scandals.

In early 1413, the same year he completed *De Ecclesia* (*The Church*), one of his most notable works, he published the aptly titled *Concerning Simony.* As implied by its title, the book was a withering commentary and investigation into the practice. A few months later, Hus took a breather from his virulent campaign against the Church and penned a book on the subject of the path to salvation. He also authored a number of aggressive treatises against his former comrades Palec and Stanislav. *World Atlas* contributor Aliasgar Abuwala described the impact of Hus' original literature: "When [Hus] switched from Latin to Czech, he developed a new orthography like simpler rules of spelling, capitalization, hyphenation, and punctuation, etc. These works are [now] considered classics of Czech literature and remain important in the evolution of the Czech language."

Notwithstanding his fugitive status, Hus is said to have slithered in and out of Prague a few times, discovering that so long as he refrained from stepping behind the pulpit, the interdict was not enforced. As if to put this theory to the test, Hus slipped into one of the local churches mid-sermon, apparently, as reported by his detractors, to hijack the pulpit. Local authorities seized the reformer mid-stride. One can only speculate as to why Hus was released, but before long, the reformer had retreated to the shadows.

In autumn of 1414, Hus received a curious letter bearing the wax seal of Sigismund of Nuremberg, King of Germany and future Holy Roman Emperor. The reformer had been invited to attend the Council of Constance, and the German king assured Hus that he need not fear because the council was just a friendly conference that simply aimed to resolve a few issues. In addition, Hus was presented with the chance to properly and civilly defend himself before the ecumenical council. Sigismund even offered to dispatch to his location a hand-picked retinue of his finest knights, who were tasked with escorting the reformer to and from the council and guaranteeing protection throughout the conference.

Although initially reluctant, Hus ultimately decided that he would be remiss if he passed up the opportunity, so in mid-October 1414, Sigismund's knights arrived at Hus' hideout and delivered him to Constance, as promised. Along the way, hundreds of the reformer's disciples emerged from their homes, jogging alongside him and cheering him on. Little did they know, this would be the last time anyone outside of the council would see him in the flesh.

Just minutes after his climactic arrival at the conference grounds, the same knights who shepherded him to Constance closed in on him and hauled him into the house of a church official. The flummoxed Hus remained captive for a period of eight days before he was relocated to the dungeon of a Dominican monastery on one of the islands off the coast of Lake Constance. To the prisoner's consternation, he remained shackled in this squalid cell, which reeked of stale air and rodent urine, for 4-6 months.

A depiction of Hus at the Council of Constance

On December 4, 1414, about two months into Hus' imprisonment, a pope-appointed committee consisting of a trio of bishops began their preliminary inquiry against the imprisoned reformer. The council, it seemed, made little effort to hide their partiality - the prosecutors, for one, were permitted to present their entire line-up of witnesses, but the disoriented defendant, who was denied a legal adviser, had to fend for himself.

The sudden deposition of Antipope John XXIII was more drama that Hus did not need. Up to this point, Hus sought solace in the visits he was tentatively granted from his friends, but the prisoner suffered yet another devastating blow as a result of the inevitable transition in power. Hus was once again relocated, this time to the Gottlieben Castle in Thurgau, Switzerland, which belonged to the Archbishop of Constance. Hus remained in the frosty and poorly lit cell of the Western Tower for 73 days, and this was presumably the most torturous chapter of Hus' imprisonment. In addition to the deprivation of virtually all human contact, chains weighed down his frail wrists and numb legs day in and day out. He was also appallingly fed, if at all, which led to malnutrition. With his immune system compromised, he became infested with disease.

The first of the official trials against Hus took place on June 5, 1415. To facilitate the process, the ailing prisoner was transferred again to a nearby Franciscan monastery, where he spent his final days on Earth. The editors of *Great Site* described the proceedings: "[Hus] acknowledged the writings on the Church against his former comrades Palec and Stanislaus as his own, and declared himself willing to recant, if errors should be proven to him. Hus conceded his veneration of Wycliffe, and said that he could only wish his soul might some time attain unto that place where Wycliffe's was. On the other hand, he denied having defended Wycliffe's doctrine of the Lord's Supper, or the forty-five articles; he had only opposed their summary condemnation. [Sigismund] admonished him to deliver himself up to the mercy of the council, as he did not desire to protect a heretic."

Hus' final trial was set for June 8, 1415. During these proceedings, the prosecutors recited to him 39 sentences, 26 of which were plucked from *De Sex Erroribus*, 7 of which came from Hus' bitter disquisition on Palec, and 6 of which came from the treatise that targeted Stanislaus. The prosecutors made certain to underscore Wycliffe's influence on Hus' literature, and the defendant was also made to explain his unauthorized induction of the three slain Hussites into martyrdom. Palec took to the stand and read aloud a passage from Chapter 21 in Hus' *De Ecclesia*: "[S]imple laymen and priests who are instructed by the grace of God can teach many people through good example and publicly contradict the lies of Antichrist but will perish with the sword. This is to be seen in the case of three laymen who opposed the deceitful helpers of Antichrist and were slain with the sword." Palec also made reference to the sermon Hus conducted following the execution of the Hussite martyrs, in which he blisteringly referred to the tragedy as "the price for calling into question papal authority."

According to witnesses, throughout the entirety of his trials, the defendant, though in poor health, remained for the most part either stoic or calm. At one point, the feeble Hus declared before the council, "I would not, for a chapel full of gold, recede from the truth."

On the fateful Saturday afternoon of July 6, 1415, Hus was given one final opportunity to recant. The prisoner, who was now so weak that he had to be physically supported, refused, effectively signing his death sentence. Thus, the ecumenical council, reportedly with no shortage of pleasure, declared the 46-year-old an "arch-heretic" and sent him on his way to the Constance Cathedral, the scene of his execution. Seven bishops stepped forth from the sidelines and encircled the battered reformer, who had crumpled to his knees. The murmuring bishops spat and called Hus a "cursed Judas" as they forcibly removed his shabby clerical robes, replacing them with robes featuring frightening demons, and sheared off tufts of his greasy, matted hair. "You have been committed to hell," the bishops told the condemned man. "May God have mercy on your soul."

A pulsing throng of thousands watched, some whistling and others weeping, as the executioners chained the reformer to a looming stake centered in a bed of kindling (supposedly including pages from Wycliffe's manuscripts). A chilling demonic headdress, its shape reminiscent of a spearhead, was then placed on his crown, most likely to match his unsettling robes.

As they adjusted the headdress, Hus' executioners repeatedly chanted, "We commit your soul to the devil!" To this, a tearful Hus craned his neck back to gaze at the heavens and responded,

"And I commit it to the most merciful Lord Jesus Christ on account of me, a miserable wretch, bore a much heavier and harsher crown of thorns. Being innocent, he was deemed deserving of the most shameful death. Therefore I, a miserable wretch and sinner, will humbly bear this much lighter, even though vilifying crown for His name and truth!"

But Hus was not done. As his executioners tightened his chains, he forced a smile and continued, "My Lord Jesus Christ was bound with a harder chain than this for my sake, and why then should I be ashamed of this rusty old thing?"

As Hus' executioners piled on the kindling, the Duke of Bavaria became so disturbed by the imminent tragedy that he exhorted the reformer to recant, only to be firmly rejected by Hus. "No, I never preached any doctrine of an evil tendency, and what I taught with my lips, I shall now seal with my blood."

Legend has it that he then turned to his executioners and quipped, "You are now going to burn a goose, but in a century, you will have a swan which you can neither roast nor boil." There are many who believe that Hus had unwittingly revealed a prophecy - just moments from death, they say, Hus had predicted the rise of Martin Luther. Even more compelling, a swan was featured in some versions of Luther's family seal.

Witnesses recorded Hus' alleged last words: "Let it be known, [with] God as my witness, that I have never taught nor preached what is attributed to me on the testimony of false witnesses. My prime intention in my preaching and all my actions has been to extricate men from sin. I am ready to die with joy in the truth of the gospel, which I have written, taught, and preached in accordance with the tradition of the Holy Doctors."

With that, the executioners set the kindling ablaze and stepped back, their faces contorting with a mixture of revulsion and horror as the flames consumed the Bohemian martyr. John Foxe, John Malham, and T. Pratt, editors of *Fox's Book of Martyrs, Or, The Acts and Monuments of the Christian Church* described the final moments of Hus in detail: "The flames were now applied to the [woodpile], when our martyr sung a hymn with so loud and cheerful a voice that he was heard through all the cracklings of the combustiles, and the noise of the multitude. At length his voice was interrupted by the severity of the flames, which soon closed his existence."

Hus' ashes were later swept up and dumped into the cold, coursing waters of the River Rhine.

In den ziten und vorhin bi langen tagen was ze
Bechein in dem lande und sunderlich ze prag
ungloub und gross ketzerie erwachsen. und

Medieval depictions of Hus' execution

The Anti-Hussite Crusade

Needless to say, even in his own time, many believed the treatment of Hus was far from fair, especially given that he had traveled to Constance with a guarantee of his safety but was instead quickly imprisoned. Sigismund was furious his pledge was broken but was persuaded to uphold the detainment to prevent Hus from preaching, so there seems to have been a presumption of his guilt from the very beginning. Then there was the fundamental question of legality. When the trial began, Pope John XXIII had abandoned the council, and the tradition of the Western Church held that only the consent of the Bishop of Rome could legitimize a general council. As recently as 1963, the Second Vatican Council lapsed and had to be recalled after another Pope John XXIII[2] had died. Constance had declared otherwise, yet there was sufficient dissent to allow a defender of Hus to argue his trial was illegal. Furthermore, Hus was not permitted to explain himself but commanded to submit to the judgment that his writings were heretical and recant them. There is no doubt that Hus admired the theology of Wycliffe – he declared so himself – and based his own teaching on it, but he was not allowed to either incriminate or exonerate himself. Then there was Sigismund, who, though not acting as judge, presided over the council that tried Hus and actively intervened during the trial. His involvement suggests the emperor was both judge and executioner. Hus' trial and execution as well as the lack of justice were likely prominent in the minds of Martin Luther and his supporters when he appeared before the Diet of Worms in 1521.

When the Bohemian nobility learned of the execution, it sent a stern letter to the council, the *Protestatio Bohemorum*. This document, dated September 2, 1415, condemned Hus' death as an attack not only against the Czech Church but the Czech nation. Further, they appealed to a future pope against the council's judgment. A league of knights and barons was formed for the protection of the Hussite reformers. It pledged to allow any priest (by which it meant the reformers) to preach freely anywhere in the kingdom and they were to be judged only by the written word of God. Any foreign ex-communication was to be considered of no account. [3]The protestors appear to have been motivated by more than spiritual considerations. Some doubtless thought of enriching themselves with the estates of the Church, and in truth, their motivations, as in any revolution, were probably mixed.[4]

Constance then decreed that promises of safe conduct made by princes did not protect heretics from the Inquisition (Session 19, September 23, 1415). This decree was likely directed at Wenceslaus, who, to avoid a split in his kingdom, adopted a non-interventionist policy. The Church also sent letters urging the Catholic authorities in Bohemia to restrain the Hussites and urge the king to intervene, and it further cited all the signatories to the *Protestatio* to appear before it.[5] Sigismund went further, hurling openly violent threats at the members of the Hussite league. As emperor-elect and overlord of his brother, Wenceslaus, he would not allow heresy in Bohemia, especially as he was next in line to its throne.

The emperor's menaces predictably incensed the reformist faction in Bohemia. Disorders broke out and many priests loyal to Constance were driven from their parishes, yet the Hussites seemed uncertain as to how to replace the ecclesiastical structure and split broadly into two factions. The more moderate Hussites who were following the teaching of Hus' disciples in Prague and stood for the administration of communion under both kinds became known as the Ultraquists or Calixtines (from the Latin *calix,* meaning "chalice"). They did not deny the doctrine of transubstantiation, nor did they wish to split entirely from the hierarchical Church. If

---

[2]Angelo Roncalli also called himself John XXIII owing to a doubt as to the legitimacy of the fifteenth century
    pope.
[3] Howard Kaminsky (2004)*A History of the Hussite Revolution* Wipf and Stock Publishers p. 145.
[4] Ibid. p. 150 – 151.
[5] Ibid., p.149.

they truly represented what Hus believed, then the Council of Constance did indeed condemn him unjustly since ultraquism was not strictly heretical. The council's enmity was based mainly on their refusal to accept its authority and their insistence that communion should be administered under both kinds. Appealing to a future pope against the council was not heretical, for the conciliar doctrine that a general council was superior to a pope was itself an innovation of Marsilius and others. A compromise might have been reached had it not been for the intransigence of Sigismund and the second major group of Hussites, the Taborites.

The Taborites were named after Tabor, the city in Bohemia that served as their base. They claimed to adhere to the teachings of Hus, though their beliefs more resembled those of the radical Protestants of the 16th century. They were Wycliffists rather than Hussites, believing the Bible alone dictated belief and morality, that clerical authority was invented, and that Christ was not substantially present in the consecrated bread and wine. Moreover, they held that Christ's reign on Earth began through their communities, in which all people were equal and everything was held in common. Both the Ultraquists and conservative Catholics regarded them as subversive, but the Taborites believed it was their duty to take arms against the enemies of Christ in preparation for His coming. One Taborite sect, known as Adamists, practiced nudity and free love in the belief that since Christ had restored man's original innocence, it was thus impossible to sin.[6]

Meanwhile, Constance worked toward healing the schism in the Western Church. In November 1417, the Church elected Cardinal Otto Colonna as pope, and he took the name Martin V. John XXIII was in prison, charged with piracy, murder, sodomy, and rape, amongst other crimes. The Roman Pope Gregory XII had acknowledged the council and then resigned, while the Avignon Pope Benedict XIII fled to Aragon where he was ignored. The schism was finally over. In May the following year, the council dispersed and Martin made his way to Rome, long-neglected and in a lamentable state of lawlessness. He accepted the council's mandate to enact certain reforms and to call another general council in five years, but he was committed to restoring papal authority. To do this, he needed to quell the unrest in Bohemia. An opportunity to do so came when Wenceslaus IV died of a heart attack on July 30, 1419, and a group of Ultraquist led by a priest, John Želivský, protested before the Prague Town Hall. Stones were thrown from the hall windows, insults were exchanged, and people stormed the building. The burgomaster and several councilors were thrown from the windows and killed.[7] This outraged and alarmed the Catholics, and upon Wenceslaus's death, civil war seemed imminent.

---

[6] Andrew Wilson (22 March 2015). "From the Observer archive, 17 March 1974: the naked truth about streaking". *The Guardian*.

[7] The event is known as the First Defenestration of Prague. Defenestration means 'ejection from a window', from the Latin *fenestratio*, 'window.' The Second Defenestration occurred in 1618 when Protestants threw the Catholic regents of Bohemia out of Prague Castle.

Martin V

Wenceslaus had not been an advocate for the Hussites, despite his early support for Hus, but he did not want them provoked into open conflict either. Sigismund, conversely, had no such qualms. The estates of Bohemia refused to recognize the succession and German Catholics were expelled from the cities and towns. The regent Sophia of Bavaria, widow of Wenceslaus IV, attempted to regain control of Prague but was forced to make a truce with the Hussites on November 13.

However, the Taborites would not accept any compromise and took control of the city under the leadership of John Žižka, a minor aristocrat and former chamberlain to Queen Sophia. Called the "One-Eyed," he had a genius for organization and tactics that would give the Hussites victory after victory. In December 1419, he attacked a Catholic-held stronghold at Nekmíř, about 100 kilometers southwest of Prague. He had only 400 infantry but succeeded in repelling a force of 2,000 infantry and cavalry. For the first time, Žižka used his famous tactic: mounting handguns on carts to create a mobile fortress.

A contemporary depiction of Žižka leading soldiers

A statue of Žižka in Tabor

In March 1420, Sigismund was assembling an army at Breslau, Silesia, and on March 20, the papal legate, Bishop Ferdinand of Lucena, read the papal bull *Omnium plasmatoris domini,* which declared a crusade against Wycliffites, Hussites, and other heretics. Four days later, Žižka's Hussites defeated but did not break a force of 2,000 knights at Sudoměř, including the military order of the Knights Hospitaller. The crusade set off under the personal command of Sigismund, and by May 3, his army was before the walls of Klodsko on the Eastern Neisse River along the Silesian/Bohemian border.

Klodzko fell without a struggle, and the town held a strategic pass through the Sudeten Mountains separating Silesia from Bohemia which would be the base for the crusaders' campaign. The army of perhaps 80,000[8], comprised mostly of Germans, royal Bohemian troops, and Hungarians, made for Prague, encountering Taborite positions but generally failing to break

---

[8] Verney, Victor (2009). *Warrior of God: Jan Zizka and the Hussite Revolution.* Frontline Books.

them. Nevertheless, the enemy was nowhere near strong enough to engage the crusader army in open battle, and it had no real trouble approaching Prague toward the end of June.

Meanwhile, Žižka was raising troops near Prague. His armies were mostly peasants armed with flails, axes and billhooks – modified agricultural implements – and gentry cavalry, with a few traditional aristocratic knights. However, they possessed certain advantages over the crusaders. Perhaps most importantly, they were fighting with the kind of religious zeal that did not easily accept surrender, and they also possessed Žižka's military genius, especially the use of the handgun (a type of primitive musket) and defensive constructions such as wagon-forts.

The Vlatava River divided medieval Prague. The Lesser Town was located on the west bank while the older settlement containing the Town Hall and the royal palace was on the east bank. Sigismund's camp was on the north bank facing the Old Town. The crusaders first attacked and took Hradcany Castle in Lesser Town, which was unprotected by the river, but this was purely a diversionary venture to draw the city's defenses while the main force crossed the Vlatava to assault the Old Town from the east. Before the assault on the Old Town could begin, the crusaders must take a palisade located on Vitkov Hill. On June 12, about 16,000 crusader knights mounted the ridge before the palisade and began the assault.

On June 14, Žižka returned to Prague with cavalry and infantry of about 3,000, and he marched to the palisade and attacked the knights on the right flank. This drove them north along the ridge toward the river, where more troops were moving toward the city wall. When the routed knights reached the river, the Prague garrison sallied out and attacked. The knights were now caught between the garrison, as well as Žižka and their advancing comrades, and the knights had no choice but to flee downhill along the river. They crashed into the oncoming troops, creating disorder and effectively halting the assault. In the confusion, many knights perished in the river. The crusaders lost between 400–500 knights, while the Hussite losses were negligible.

Hdracany Castle and Vysehrad, to the south of the Old Town, remained in the crusaders' hands, and Sigismund planned a second assault from these strongholds. However, his plan was discovered after one of his couriers was captured, and Žižka attacked and captured Vysehrad on November 1, 1420. By now, Sigismund reluctantly recognized that he could not take Prague. Leaving a garrison at Hdracany which held out until June 1421, he lifted the siege and withdrew his army first into Catholic-controlled Moravia and from there into Hungary.

The Hussites had repelled the crusade against them but now they had to resolve on what to do next. The moderate Ultraquists ultimately wished to reconcile with Rome (albeit on their terms), but this was not acceptable to the Taborites, who would never accept Rome's authority. A compromise was reached in the form of the Four Articles of Prague. It was far from being a statement of shared belief; instead, it was a list of conditions for a *modus Vivendi* – an agreement to live peacefully with the emperor and with each other. The Four Articles of Prague stated the following:

1) The word of God was to be preached freely by the clergy throughout Bohemia and in an orderly manner.

2) The eucharist was to be administered under both kinds to the laity.

3) The clergy were to be deprived of their temporal goods and made to live after the manner of Christ's apostles.

4) All mortal (serious) sins, especially public ones, were to be denounced and punished by the appropriate authority.

The articles were acceptable to the Taborites, for there was nothing in them that could offend Wycliffite sensibilities, and the Ultraquists were pleased because it contained no heretical statement to which the pope or emperor could object.

Divisions and the Council of Basel

While they had reached an agreement of sorts amongst themselves, the Hussites were not overly hopeful the Catholic powers would accept them. Neither the Catholic Church nor the emperor could allow priests to preach without limitation or oversight. The Council of Constance had already forbidden communion under both kinds; the Church in Bohemia would never willingly renounce its riches, and the denunciations of both public and private morality demanded by the reformers went far beyond even the remit of the Inquisition. Sigismund and the papal legates rejected the Four Articles. In May, he called a diet of the German princes at Nuremberg to endorse Martin V's proclamation of a second crusade.

In June 1421, a representative assembly of the Bohemian nation rejected the German emperor as king and elected a council to manage Bohemian affairs, without agreeing on who should be king. While they deliberated, a crusader army composed mostly of Saxons unsuccessfully assailed the Hussite stronghold of Zatec in northwestern Bohemia in August. Emperor Sigismund, invading through the White Mountains from Hungary, arrived in December with 2000 men and was defeated by John Žižka at the Battle of Deutschbrod (Havlíčkův Brod) on January 10, 1422. The Hussites had only 400 men and 12 wagon forts but managed to inflict 500 casualties and take the imperial supply train.

After repelling the second wave of crusaders, the Bohemians returned to the question of the government. Under the influence of Žižka, the representative assembly offered the crown to the Poland's King Vladislaus II, but he would not accept the Four Articles. Next they invited Vytautas, Grand Duke of Lithuania, to sit on the throne, and he accepted on the condition that the Hussites seek reconciliation with Rome and sent Prince Sigismund Korybut, a nephew of Vladislaus, to serve as regent. It seemed the Hussites had won their freedom, but there were still enormous differences between the factions to be resolved.

The invitation divided the Bohemian nation. The Ultraquist nobility and burghers of Prague welcomed the arrival of his regent and the prospect of reconciliation with Rome, but he must have been aware of the near impossibility of that task. Neither Martin V nor Emperor Sigismund had given the slightest indication that peace was possible. The moderate Ultraquists believed it was theoretically possible, but for most of the Wycliffites of Tabor, submission to Rome was out of the question.

Despite the Taborite skepticism, enthusiasm amongst the Ultraquists was high. Burgrave Čeněk of Wartenberg, one of the highest-ranking of the Bohemian nobility, anticipated Sigismund's arrival by leading a force of 3,000 cavalry, artillery, and wagons against John Žižka and 3,000 radical Hussites at Hořice on April 27, 1423. The Hussites constructed a wagon fort on the top of a hill and allowed the enemy to exhaust themselves before charging down the slopes to deliver the *coup de grace*. Shortly after, Korybut arrived in Prague with 2,500 Poles to general rejoicing, but after failing to break the Hussites and pressure from the pope and Emperor Sigismund, he returned to Lithuania in late December. Since there was no help available beyond Bohemia, the Ultraquists concluded an armistice with Žižka.

Meanwhile, Martin V had renewed the crusade, but the response was weak because the Ottoman Turks were attacking Hungary and the German princes were at odds with Sigismund. Eric, King of Denmark, Norway, and Sweden landed in Germany with a sizeable force, but seeing the lack of enthusiasm there, he turned back.

In June 1424, Sigismund Korybut returned with a small army but this time without the approbation of Vytautas. He installed himself in Prague, replaced the Ultraquist leaders, and brokered a peace between Prague and Tabor, for which he was excommunicated by the pope. With the peace established, Žižka could plan an invasion of Catholic-held Moravia but died of the plague (October 11) before he could carry it out. An attempt by the new Taborite leadership to execute the plan failed due to internal divisions.

Martin V was now keen to take advantage of Žižka's death and Hussite divisions by ordering another attack. The political landscape in Germany seemingly favored another Bohemian invasion, especially as Hussite armies were invading Saxony and Silesia, and some 13000[9] crusaders invaded northern Bohemia in June 1426. Korybut held out the hand of friendship to the priest, Prokop the Bald, who had assumed leadership of the Taborites, and together they met the invaders with 11000 men and 500 war wagons. Following proven tactics, the Hussites set up their fortification on a hill overlooking Aussig (Ústí nad Labem), a mountainous town at the confluence of the Elbe and Bilina Rivers. On June 16, the Thuringian and Saxon knights charged the fort and broke through by cleaving through the chains that linked the wagons, likely with axes. They discovered a second line of shields and infantry but no cavalry, and so were confident of victory. However, the Hussite cavalry had left the fort and was swinging around upon the knights. Caught between the cavalry and heavy projectile fire, the crusaders routed and dispersed

---

[9] Medieval chroniclers state 70 000, but this is almost certainly an exaggeration. ČORNEJ, Petr; BĚLINA, Pavel (1993). *Slavné bitvy naší historie* (in Czech). Praha: Marsyas.

into the nearby villages. An estimated 4000 crusaders, including around 500 noblemen perished, though their commander, Bono of Vitzthum, escaped. Thus ended the third Hussite crusade, in much the same manner as the others.

The Hussite attacks into Germany had finally galvanized the princes into action, but only if it was done on their own terms. In 1424 the Prince-electors (the seven magnates who elected the emperor) pledged themselves to speak with one voice not only against the Hussites but the emperor as well. If Sigismund was determined to reconcile with the Ultraquists (and the Ultraquists still wanted reconciliation with the pope and the empire), he was now powerless to act. Martin V, intent on asserting papal authority, proved unapproachable - in 1427, he appointed the English cardinal, Henry Beaufort, as his legate to Germany. Sigismund commanded him to organize yet another crusade and personally lead it into battle in Sigismund's name. However, the crusaders had learned from the failures of previous attempts, the result of the commanders insisting on employing traditional tactics of medieval chivalry against a very unconventional enemy.

The age of knights was fading, as had long been obvious – not only through the Hussite wars but in other conflicts where heavy cavalry was being overcome by infantry armed with pikes, halberds, and firearms. As early as 1346, the English's victory against the French at Crecy had been decided by men-at-arms and archers, not heavy cavalry. In 1396, when Sigismund was king only of Hungary, he lead a battle against the Turks at Nicopolis in Bulgaria, where the knights of Europe were decimated. That battle sent a demoralizing tremor throughout Europe.

Cardinal Beaufort decided the crusade would adopt the wagon-forts tactic of the Hussites which had been so decisive for them in earlier battles, but the Battle of Tachov (August 3-4, 1427) near the western border of Bohemia proved that the Hussites were masters of the wagon-forts. Cardinal Beaufort, Frederick I of Brandenburg, and Otto, Archbishop of Trier, set up fortifications to the north of Tachov with about 25,000 men, and Prokop was nearby with about 15,000 infantry, 1,500 light cavalry, and 200 battlewagons. The crusaders sent a cavalry of 3,000 ahead to slow Prokop's advance and secure more time to consolidate their defenses, but they returned without engaging the enemy. The lack of engagement along with the Hussites' well-known reputation had a demoralizing effect on the entire army. When Prokop finally arrived on August 4, most of the crusader forces had left camp and were retiring toward Tachov. The remaining rear-guard was easily smashed, and Tachov capitulated on August 11.

A depiction of papal legate Henry Beaufort trying to halt fleeing crusaders after the battle

After Tachov, the Hussites resolved to take the fight to their enemies and invaded enemy territory. Raiders devastated Saxony, Bavaria, Hungary, Brandenburg, Silesia, and Lusatia, not with the intent of conquest but to discourage these lands from supplying men for the crusades. In Silesia, they established permanent bases that enabled the sacking of the entire province. The Hussites called these expeditions "beautiful rides."

Despite these successes, there seemed to be no road to peace, and Sigismund Korybut made overtures to the emperor. The Taborite leaders, fearing that he was about to betray them, had him arrested and imprisoned at Valdštejn Castle, near Turnov in northern Bohemia. The removal of the Ultraquist leader left the Taborites firmly in control of the movement, and Prokop used the "beautiful rides" to spread Hussite ideology. It will be remembered that the Taborites and other radical Hussites advocated the abolishment of all authority in preparation for the Second Coming of Christ, and they believed laying waste to the corrupt world was the work of God.

In early 1429, Sigismund and a group of German princes surprisingly invited Prokop and other Hussite leaders for talks at Pressburg (Bratislava). Until then, Sigismund had resolutely refused to negotiate, but the acceptance by Prokop is even more surprising, though he possibly realized that the war could not go on forever. Remembering the fate of Hus, he and the other Hussite notables arrived on April 3 with a strong military escort.

Sigismund proposed the cessation of conflict until a new general council – due to convene at Basel in 1431 - decided the dogmatic differences between the belligerents. In the meantime, all lands seized by the Hussites would be returned to the Church. The Hussites agreed to accept Sigismund's nominal sovereignty over Bohemia if he agreed to accept the reform of the Church and the Four Articles. They did not expect Sigismund to break with the pope; they only sought the Bohemian Church's freedom.

The Hussites seemed amenable to attending a council, but Sigismund could not immediately accept their terms. Furthermore, the truce might have lasted had Pope Martin V, who was reluctant to surrender the government of the Church to a council, renewed the holy war against them. Sigismund needed the pope to crown him emperor in Rome (he was still only Emperor-elect or "King of the Romans"), so he reluctantly took up the sword again.

As a result, a large number of German, Bohemian Catholic, Hungarian, and Italian crusaders, possibly as many as 120,000 men, invaded southwestern Bohemia under the command of Frederick of Brandenburg's and Martin V's legate, Cardinal Cesarini. Prokop and Sigismund Korybut – released from prison – met them at Domažlice with 55,000 on August 8, 1431, and the ensuing encounter was not so much a battle as a massacre. The Hussites approached singing their battle song, "Ye who are warriors of God," which contained the following verse:

> "Do not fear your enemies, nor gaze upon their number,
>
> Keep the Lord in your hearts; for Him fight on,
>
> And before enemies you need not flee."

The sound of their singing, the sight of their confident approach, and no doubt their reputation instilled such terror that the crusaders began to panic before even giving battle. Soldiers broke position en masse, leaving their hapless commanders no choice but to follow them. Those few who remained fought the Hussites for several hours before being overwhelmed. Their sacrifice allowed the bulk of the crusaders to escape, albeit in irretrievable disorder. Several thousand perished, and artillery, war wagons, and supply trains were captured.

A depiction of Cardinal Cesarini retreating

Domažlice convinced the Catholic princes and even the princes of the Church that Bohemia could not be brought back into the fold by force of arms. The Council of Basel issued an invitation to the Hussite leaders to meet with its envoys in May 1432 at Cheb, just inside the Bohemian border with Saxony. In the history of the Catholic Church, the meeting is extraordinary, as the conciliar legates invited the Hussites to attend the council. Previously, those judged heretics appeared before an inquisition and accepted its judgment, but this time, they were being invited to return to the Church willingly, presaging to some degree the open attitude of the Second Vatican Council (1962–1965) toward non-Catholic Christians. The Catholics of 1432 were not so liberal, but they did recognize that the traditional methods of condemnation and crusade had failed, and the council promised them freedom of worship and the liberty to advance their case. It was in effect admitting that the condemnation and execution of Hus had been unnecessary, if not unjust.

Sigismund received the envoys of Prokop kindly and agreed to aid the Hussites toward reconciliation. The main opponent to peace, Martin V, had died in February 1431, but the new Pope Eugene IV was at loggerheads with the council, whose supreme authority he would not acknowledge. Sigismund was still not crowned emperor, so he worked to reconcile the pope with the council, which resulted in delayed reconciliation. In 1433, Sigismund was finally crowned emperor, and in January 1433 a Hussite legation was at last received by the council fathers at Basel. True to their word, they permitted Hussite preachers to expound – vehemently – on the Four Articles. The Catholics replied, and the debate was not without acrimony. Nevertheless, they were communicating without threatening to burn each other. In February, Cardinal Cesarini invited the Hussites to acknowledge the legitimacy of the council and to work with it. This was not a demand of submission like the Council of Constance had made – the safe conducts and expressions of good will were still in force –but the issue divided the Hussites and they agreed to retire to Prague to consider their position. In winter, they returned but failed to offer any leeway on the Four Articles.

Eugene IV

In Bohemia, there was a growing sentiment that blamed Prokop and the radical Taborites for failing to reach an agreement with the council, which was not entirely fair since Prokop had initiated the talks in the first place. There were some in Basel who encouraged the rift, and civil war broke out. The failure of Prokop to capture Pilsen was a major blow to the Taborites and presaged the even more calamitous defeat at Lipany (May 30, 1434). In that encounter, both Ultraquists and Taborites numbered over 10,000 men, and after a useless exchange of cannon fire, the Taborites were surprised to see the enemy withdrawing. Prokop ordered an attack, but he realized too late he had been deceived by a false retreat, an old battle strategy that had destroyed many armies. More than a thousand Taborites perished, including Prokop himself, and after the battle, 700 of the Taborite survivors were taken and burned alive.

The Council of Basel could scarcely contain its joy, and it ordered the traditional *Te Deum* sung in thanksgiving. It was so much easier to deal with the Ultraquists alone for they desired reconciliation more earnestly than the radicals. With the extreme Wycliffites sidelined – though not eliminated entirely – the Bohemian Diet ratified the Compacts of Basel on July 5, 1436. By these agreements, priests were authorized to administer communion under both kinds to the laity of Bohemia and Moravia, overturning the ruling of the Council of Constance. The other three articles were effectively abandoned, much to the disgust of the Taborites and other factions who believed 25 years of blood and sacrifice had been for nothing. Despite this, they begrudgingly accepted the peace.

As *Te Deums* were sung at Basel and Prague and excommunications were rescinded (John Hus remained anathematized), peace returned to Bohemia. Emperor Sigismund could at last enter Prague as King of Bohemia. There remained bones of contention, however, as would be expected after a lengthy conflict. John of Rokycan, the prelate who governed the Bohemian Church during the war, was not accepted by the council as Archbishop of Prague since he had been elected by the Diet and not by the chapter if cathedral clerics. Further, it became clear the council fathers were willing to *allow* communion under both kinds but it was not mandated, and Pope Eugene did not seem to accept even that.[10] The entire process of negotiating with heretics began to be called into question when the pope and council argued over the issue of papal authority. In January 1438, Eugene IV convened a council on his own authority at Ferrara and excommunicated the members of the Council of Basel, who refused to attend. In turn, they deposed and replaced him with the Count of Savoy, Amadeus VII, who accepted the election as Felix V without even being a priest. The primary concern of Eugene IV's council at Florence was the union with the Eastern Orthodox Church, while Felix struggled to gain recognition. The 10-year schism ended with Felix's abdication.

When the Church faced internal squabbles, the problems posed by the Bohemian Church were barely addressed, but in 1449, Pope Nicholas V closed the Council of Florence, determined to rule the Church himself. If the leaders of the Bohemian Church thought they had achieved their freedom, they were sadly mistaken.

Nicholas V

---

[10]Thomas M. Izbicki and Gerald Christiansen (2017) *A companion to the Council of Basel*, Brill p.277.

The Last Hussite Wars

In 1437, the year after Bohemia ratified the Compacts of Basel, Emperor Sigismund died and was succeeded in Bohemia by the Margrave of Moravia, Albert of Habsburg, designated heir during the Hussite wars. He was also King of Hungary and later elected King of the Romans, but the Bohemian nobility, who demanded a voice in the choice of monarch, refused to recognize him. His attempt to conquer Bohemia was thwarted, but after his death in 1439 his young son, Ladislaus, claimed the throne.

Ladislaus became a focus for the elements of the Bohemian Church who wanted closer cooperation with Rome, and while the Czech nobility was divided, they strove to avoid bloodshed. Unfortunately, it soon became clear that war could not be avoided, and in 1448, the Hussites (now consisting almost entirely of the moderate Ultraquists) rallied around George of Poděbrady, a prominent nobleman who defeated the papist nobles. At first he was confirmed regent by the minders of the 8-year old Ladislaus, who was crowned in Prague on October 28, 1453, but Ladislaus died four years later and George of Poděbrady was elected king by the Czech nobility. Rumors circulated that George of Poděbrady had murdered the king, but recent research indicates that Ladislaus died of leukemia.[11]

A medieval depiction of George of Poděbrady

---

[11] Pálosfalvi, Tamás (2002). "V. László". In Kristó, Gyula (ed.). *Magyarország vegyes házi királyai* [The Kings of Various Dynasties of Hungary] (in Hungarian). Szukits Könyvkiadó. pp. 149..

After Poděbrady's assumption of power, Pope Nicholas V attempted to seize control of the Bohemian Church by demanding it renounce the Compacts of Basel, which he believed had been illegally or dishonorably wrested from Eugene IV. Regardless, the Compacts had permitted communion under both kinds, not mandated it, so to the pope, the Roman Church was fully entitled to restrict the practice as it judged proper.[12] The reply of the Czechs was measured but firm, as they asserted the pope and his advisers did not understand the nature of the Compacts. Furthermore, the pope had no authority to overrule a general council, and Scripture, not clerical authority, was the supreme judge.

The last argument rankled Rome especially. According to Catholic teaching, the meaning of Scripture needed to be authoritatively interpreted, so a declaration of *Sola Scriptura* was a declaration against the magisterial power of the Church. The papacy became more and more convinced that Basel had erred grievously in negotiating with heretics, and in 1455, a list of 70 articles were drawn up insisting the unrecognized Archbishop of Prague, Rokycana, was a heretic. In 1462, Nicholas V's successor, Pope Pius II, explicitly declared the Compacts of Basel null and void, and he declared the prohibitions of the Council of Constance were still in effect. This came after a botched attempt to steal the original copy of the Compacts of Basel stored in Prague. The repudiation of the Compacts was in fact part of a broader papal strategy of annulling conciliar authority.

---

[12] Ibid.

Pope Pius II

George of Poděbrady's response was firm but measured - he had no desire to reopen old wounds and aimed to peacefully govern both Ultraquists and papists. His people called him "King of Two Peoples" on account of his just and prudent rule, though he did punish the Taborites in order to avoid provoking the pope. If Pius sensed open heresy in Bohemia, he would doubtlessly declare a crusade and use it to conquer the Ultraquists. George of Poděbrady's efforts to appear as a prince dedicated to the peace of Christendom broke new ground in a radical proposal to create a federation of Christian states with a common parliament, which, if implemented, might have resembled the modern European Union. Its ostensible goal was to drive the Ottoman Turks, who had conquered most of the Balkans, from Europe. The *Tractatus pacis toti Christianitati fiendae* ("Treaty on the Establishment of Peace throughout Christendom") was seriously considered but not seriously entered into, and the pragmatic George likely realized it could never succeed; after all, neither the emperor nor the pope could subscribe to a European order that did not need them. Historians have suggested the plan was at least in part a cover for making alliances in the event of war with the pope.[13] If so, he succeeded, for he secured an alliance with King Louis XI of France in 1464.[14]

In 1465, Pius II's successor, Pope Paul II, proved even more recalcitrant toward the Hussites. He saw the *Tractatus* as an invitation to apostasy and commanded George of Poděbrady to appear in Rome to answer charges of heresy. When he failed to attend, Paul released his subjects from their oaths of allegiance to George of Poděbrady and excommunicated him. Furthermore, the pope gave his blessing to a league of papist noblemen ready to execute the sentence of deposition. The crusade that the majority of Bohemians had striven to avoid was now upon them.

The 21-year old King of Hungary, Matthias of Hunyadi, was quick to claim the vacant crown of Bohemia and, urged on by Emperor Frederick III, declared war on March 31, 1468. He countered a Czech attack in Austria and then in 1469 invaded Moravia and Silesia, both of which formed part of the Bohemian kingdom. At the same time, Hungary's Ottoman enemy, Mehmed II, was fighting a war in Asia Minor. An ideal opportunity to attack the Turks in Europe was lost for the sake of a dubious crusade against Christians who had not actually broken with Rome. The combined armies of Matthias and the Bohemian papists, commanded by Zdeněk of Šternberk, were encircled by George at Vilemov in central Bohemia. Matthias negotiated an agreement whereby he would intercede for Bohemia with the pope in return for an armistice. He was true to his word, though given what he stood to lose, doubt should be thrown on his motives, and in April the papal legates met with George at Olomouc. Negotiations failed, and the truce had only given time for George's enemies to take action. On May 3, the Catholic nobles elected Matthias as King of Bohemia.

Most Bohemians repudiated the election, but Matthias was accepted in Silesia and Moravia. Matthias counterattacked, expelled the Hungarians from Silesia, and routed the Hungarian army at the Battle of Uherský Brod close to the Hungarian border on November 2. Matthias lacked funds, and no other powers had joined the crusade. Frederick III accused Matthias of avoiding the Turkish menace and the Hungarian nobility was opposed. On March 22, 1471 George died, and the Bohemian Estates elected Ladislaus II, nephew of the young Ladislaus, King of Bohemia. Paul II refused to recognize the election and confirmed the crown on the head of Matthias Corvinus.

The politics of the crusade were becoming increasingly complex, and the religious element had become irrelevant. The war was clearly a tool of revenge for the papacy and of ambition for the king of Hungary. To make the situation more tragic, a group of Hungarian barons offered the crown of Hungary to Casimir, the younger son of Casimir IV of Poland, and Polish troops rampaged through Silesia. Frederick III joined Casimir and attacked Hungary from his Austrian estates. The Turks also took advantage of Matthias' vulnerability, raiding deep into the

---

[13] Norman Housley (2012) *Crusading and the Ottomsn Threat 1453 – 1503* OUP Oxford p.58.

[14] Louis did not participate in the war that followed, though his friendship with George possibly prevented the German princes from attacking Bohemia.

Hungarian plains and seizing border forts. The Bohemian heartland remained free of Hungarian troops, and in 1478, a war-weary Matthias signed the Treaty of Brno with the envoys of Vladislaus II. The latter agreed to cede Silesia, Moravia, and the adjacent province of Lusatia to Matthias with the proviso that he could buy those lands back when Matthias died.

The treaty did not deal with the religious question, which had been all but forgotten. In fact, Pope Sixtus IV began referring to Ladislaus as a faithful son. Ultraquists and papists in Bohemia settled down to a state of mutual toleration, confirmed by an agreement at Kutna Hora in 1485. The papacy was not satisfied but was prepared to accept the situation to focus on other problems, namely the onslaught of Turks into Europe, the growing power of France and Spain, the degeneration of the Holy Roman Empire, and even the challenges to its own temporal authority in central Italy.

Religious peace remained until the House of Habsburg inherited the crown of Bohemia in 1526. During the reign of Ferdinand I, who was also King of Hungary and in 1556 became the Holy Roman Emperor, the majority of Bohemia was still Ultraquist, but Lutheranism was making inroads. His brother, Emperor Charles V, was raising troops to go to war against the Protestant princes of Germany, and Ferdinand attempted to gain support from the Estates of Bohemia. An alliance of Ultraquists and Lutherans resisted him, and in putting down this revolt, he empowered Catholic nobility and clergy while revoking many of the freedoms accorded the Hussites. After Charles was forced to accept a religious settlement at the Peace of Augsburg (1555), his successor, Maximilian I, felt obliged to accept the same for Bohemia. The 1575 *Confessio Bohemica*, presented to the Habsburg monarchs, was a statement of belief subscribed to by the Ultraquists, radicals, Lutherans and Calvinists. The Confession indicated that many of the Ultraquists had shifted from the positions of the 15th century Ultraquist Hussites and probably Hus himself, particularly in regard to the nature of the eucharist, and it contained no reference to the Compacts of Basel or the Four Articles. The old Hussite demand that Christians be allowed to drink from the chalice was by this time taken up by all Protestants, and so there was little to distinguish them in the eyes of the Catholic authorities from the disciples of Luther, Calvin, and Zwingli.

Between 1545 and 1563, the Roman Catholic Council of Trent met to answer the Protestant Reformation and enact long-needed reforms. The popes had been reluctant to convene a council, fearing that, as at Constance, Basel, and Florence, it would attempt to make them subservient to its will. By this point, however, the age of conciliarism had passed, as had the consciousness of European unity that animated it. The Protestants were invited to attend with safe conducts and were promised to be allowed to address the council, as the Hussites had been invited at Basel. The Protestants refused, partly because they feared condemnation and persecution but also because they knew the case against them had already been decided. In their absence, the council addressed the question of communion under both kinds, pronouncing: "If any one denies, that, in the venerable sacrament of the Eucharist, the whole Christ is contained under each species, and under every part of each species, when separated; let him be anathema."[15]

On this point, the council confirmed the teaching of Basel – the taking of the chalice – though it was not strictly necessary to fulfill the biblical command of Christ to eat His body and drink His blood, since the entirety of Christ was present in either kind. The prohibition remained in effect precisely to counter the heresy that held the contrary notion. Nevertheless, Rome granted dispensations from the law to allow bishops in the Holy Roman Empire (of which Bohemia was a subject state) to grant the chalice to the laity as an incentive for Catholics to remain in their parishes. In the minds of many Catholic prelates, the permission was most useful to bring the Hussites back into the fold,[16] but as it turned out, it appeased neither Protestant nor Hussite.

The Hussites and Catholic authorities came to violent blows for the last time in 1618, when the fiercely Catholic Ferdinand of Habsburg was king. The Bohemian Estates resisted his efforts to impose Catholicism, and in an action reminiscent of the killing of the town councilors in 1419, Ferdinand's regents were ejected through the window of the chancellery at Prague. The Estates then elected the Protestant Elector, Frederick of the Palatinate, king in Ferdinand's place. The war between Catholics and Protestants that followed may be considered the last anti-Hussite crusade, and in a sense it initiated the horrendous bloodletting in Germany that was the Thirty Years War. The Czech army was crushed by the Habsburg forces at the Battle of White Mountain (November 8, 1620) and Frederick fled. Ferdinand, now Holy Roman Emperor, forbade the practice of Ultraquism and Protestantism: its adherents could either convert or leave the country. Most converted, with the remainder establishing communities in Germany.

With the crushing of Hussitism in Bohemia came the end of Czech nationalism, which would not be revived until the last years of the 18th century. Churches espousing the more radical beliefs of Hussitism still exist - in 1920, a group of Catholics in Czechoslovakia withdrew from Rome to form the Czechoslovak Hussite Church, which "occupies the middle ground between the essence of the Catholic Church (liturgy and the seven sacraments) and the principles of the Protestant churches (teaching and order)."[17]

In 2011, the Czechoslovak Hussite Church had just under 40000 members in the Czech Republic.[18]

The Legacy of the Hussite Wars

Historians often draw a comparison between the Hussite movement of the 15th century and the

---

[15] Session Xiii, Canon III.

[16] James Brodrick, S.J., *St. Peter Canisius* (Chicago: Loyola Univ. Press, 1962), p.547.

[17] "Czechoslovak Hussite Church", World Council of Churches https://www.oikoumene.org/member-churches/czechoslovak-hussite-church.

[18] Waybackmachine https://web.archive.org/web/20131104224923/http://www.czso.cz/sldb2011/eng/redakce.nsf/i/tab_7_2_population_by_religious_belief_and_by_regions/%24File/PVCR072_ENG.pdf.

Protestant Reformation of the 16th century, viewing the first as the precursor of the second. At a cursory glance that assertion seems logical, but the relationship between Hussitism and Protestantism is more nuanced. The Hussite movement united a variety of groups with disparate views, ranging from those differing little from mainstream Catholicism to radical anti-social millennialism. This makes reading and understanding Hussite history challenging, and while the Hussite Wars were dominated by the main two factions, the Ultraquists and the Taborites, the Hussites were not a binary group. There were multiple confessions, especially along the more radical spectrum, but they were united by their Czech nationality and their agreement on the Four Articles of Prague.

It is doubtful that Hus intended the Bohemian reform movement that took his name to radicalize as it did. It does not appear he entirely repudiated the authority of the Church and protested at Basel that his teachings, though borrowing heavily from Wycliffe, were actually orthodox. Even to his death, he protested that he had not preached anything heretical. "God is my witness that the things charged against me I never preached," he declared after his condemnation. This stands in stark contrast with Martin Luther, who, when challenged on his writings at the Diet of Worms in 1521, answered, "Unless I am convinced by the testimony of the Scriptures or by clear reason (for I do not trust either in the pope or in councils alone, since it is well known that they have often erred and contradicted themselves), I am bound by the Scriptures I have quoted and my conscience is captive to the Word of God. I cannot and will not recant anything, since it is neither safe nor right to go against conscience. May God help me. Amen."[19] Luther denied the authority of both pope and council, whereas Hus appealed to the council to defend what he regarded as the work of God.[20]

If the beliefs and practices of the moderate Ultraquists are evidence of Hus' attitude, it would seem to confirm that he did not wish to create a movement that broke entirely with the Roman Church. Until their near extinction in the early 17th century, the Ultraquists maintained the Roman liturgy with few variations, aside from the fact it was done in the Czech language instead of Latin. They did not deny the substantial presence of Christ in the eucharist, nor did they repudiate the Catholic doctrine on priestly ordination, as Luther and other Protestant leaders did. In fact, the reason the first Hussite Archbishop of Prague, Rokycana, remained unordained was because a lawfully constituted bishop could not be found to perform the ceremony. Furthermore, when the Calvinist Frederick of the Palatinate was crowned king in Prague Cathedral. he was dispirited to find that the church and coronation ceremony were almost unchanged since the coronation of Wenceslaus IV in 1363.

It appears the Ultraquists drew their strength not from a Lutheran-like spirit which wished to overturn the existing order, but from a sincere desire to reform the existing structures of the

[19] Brecht, Martin. *Martin Luther: His Road to Reformation 1483–1521* (vol 1, 1985) (1999), p. 460.
[20] Schaff, Philip *(1953)*. *"Huss, John, Hussites"*. *The New Schaff-Herzog Encyclopedia of Religious Knowledge* p. 257.

Church. In fact, such an aspiration was not endemic to 15th century Bohemia but was prevalent throughout the Catholic world. The ideas that the Church should renounce its wealth, the pope should act as a father and not a lord, and that matters affecting the universal Church should be managed by pope and council came not only from the mouth of Hus but from respected leaders such as Cardinal Marsilius of Padua, Thomas a Kempis, and William Ockham. Indeed, the very council that condemned Hus and his followers was born in large part out of desire for reform. The tragedy was that the Council of Constance acted in the traditional manner by condemning what it saw as a heterodox movement and declaring a crusade against it. Even so, the Council of Basel broke ground by opening a true dialogue with the Hussites, even if it only did so because the crusade had failed.

Ironically, the Catholic Church today has moved to a position that the Hussites might have accepted. The Second Vatican Council made the government of the Church more collegial, with the pope and bishops working together, and there is now open dialogue between the Catholic Church and other denominations and faiths. Sacred worship is conducted in the language of the people, while communion under both kinds is not only allowed but encouraged, and the written word of God enjoys an elevated place in worship. Clerics are not forbidden wealth, but its acquisition is discouraged.

Given all that, in a sense it could be argued that the degree to which the Catholic Church has reformed and opened itself to its internal critics and non-Catholics made the long wars against the Hussites even more unnecessary.

Online Resources

Other books about Christianity by Charles River Editors

Other books about Hus on Amazon

Bibliography

Abuwala, A. (2017, June 5). Jan Hus - Important Figures In History. Retrieved May 3, 2019, from https://www.worldatlas.com/articles/jan-hus-important-figures-in-history.html

Allen, J. L., Jr. (2009, September 27). Benedict XVI confronts the ghost of Jan Hus. Retrieved May 3, 2019, from https://www.ncronline.org/blogs/ncr-today/benedict-xvi-confronts-ghost-jan-hus

Bartos, F. M., & Spinka, M. (2019, January 30). Jan Hus. Retrieved May 3, 2019, from https://www.britannica.com/biography/Jan-Hus

Butler, D., & Floyd, D. F. (2004, Winter). John Wycliffe: Setting the Stage for Reform. Retrieved May 3, 2019, from https://www.vision.org/john-wycliffe-setting-stage-reform-381

Carlin, M. (2017). The Great Schism; Jan Hus. Retrieved May 3, 2019, from https://people.uwm.edu/carlin/the-great-schism-jan-hus/

Cavendish, R. (2015, May 5). John Wycliffe condemned as a heretic. Retrieved May 3, 2019, from https://www.historytoday.com/archive/john-wycliffe-condemned-heretic

Coffman, E. (2016). Jan Hus: Did You Know? Retrieved May 3, 2019, from https://www.christianitytoday.com/history/issues/issue-68/jan-hus-did-you-know.html

Curits, K., Ph.D. (2010, April 28). John Hus: Faithful unto Death. Retrieved May 3, 2019, from https://www.christianity.com/church/church-history/timeline/1201-1500/john-hus-faithful-unto-death-11629878.html

Easter, J. (2012, November 29). A Biography of Jan Hus. Retrieved May 3, 2019, from https://www.academia.edu/6726032/A_Biography_of_Jan_Hus

Editors, B. S. (2017). Persecution of John Huss. Retrieved May 3, 2019, from https://www.biblestudytools.com/history/foxs-book-of-martyrs/persecution-of-john-huss.html

Editors, C. H. (1983). John Wycliffe. Retrieved May 3, 2019, from https://www.christianitytoday.com/history/people/moversandshakers/john-wycliffe.html

Editors, C. H. (2000). John Huss: Pre-Reformation Reformer. Retrieved May 3, 2019, from https://www.christianitytoday.com/history/people/martyrs/john-huss.html

Editors, C. U. (2003). How was executed Jan Hus Peter from Mladonovic: Passion-play of Master Jan Hus. Retrieved May 3, 2019, from http://www.columbia.edu/~js322/misc/hus-eng.html

Editors, C. H. (2013). Christian History Timeline: Jan Hus—Reform and Resistance in Hussite Bohemia. Retrieved May 3, 2019, from https://christianhistoryinstitute.org/magazine/article/jan-hus-timeline

Editors, C. O. (2014). St. Lawrence, Deacon and Martyr. Retrieved May 3, 2019, from St. Lawrence, Deacon and Martyr

Editors, C. H. (2017). #302: John Hus, Reformer of Bohemia. Retrieved May 3, 2019, from https://christianhistoryinstitute.org/study/module/hus

Editors, C. T. (2018, August 10). St Lawrence: The Christian martyr who died telling a joke. Retrieved May 3, 2019, from https://www.christiantoday.com/article/st-lawrence-the-christian-martyr-who-died-telling-a-joke/130179.htm

Editors, C. W. (2019, February 9). Konrád Waldhauser. Retrieved May 3, 2019, from https://cs.wikipedia.org/wiki/Konrád_Waldhauser

Editors, E. C. (2004). Jan Hus. Retrieved May 3, 2019, from https://www.encyclopedia.com/people/literature-and-arts/german-literature-biographies/jan-hus

Editors, E. B. (2012). Transubstantiation. Retrieved May 3, 2019, from https://www.britannica.com/topic/transubstantiation

Editors, F. P. (2017, May 25). John Huss Biography. Retrieved May 3, 2019, from https://www.thefamouspeople.com/profiles/john-huss-87.php

Editors, G. S. (2016). John Hus. Retrieved May 3, 2019, from https://www.greatsite.com/timeline-english-bible-history/john-hus.html

Editors, G. S. (2016). John Wycliffe. Retrieved May 3, 2019, from https://www.greatsite.com/timeline-english-bible-history/john-wycliffe.html

Editors, H. (2012). The Medieval Relic Trade. Retrieved May 3, 2019, from http://hoaxes.org/archive/permalink/the_medieval_relic_trade/

Editors, H. P. (2015, July 14). Remembering Jan Hus. Retrieved May 3, 2019, from https://www.history.pcusa.org/blog/2015/07/remembering-jan-hus

Editors, K. U. (2007). The Movarian Church: John Hus (Jan Hus). Retrieved May 3, 2019, from https://www2.kenyon.edu/projects/margin/hus.htm

Editors, L. P. (2017). The Swan. Retrieved May 3, 2019, from http://lutheranpress.com/the-swan/

Editors, M. T. (2017). Peasants, Serfs and Farmers. Retrieved May 3, 2019, from https://www.medievaltimes.com/teachers-students/materials/medieval-era/people.html

Editors, N. W. (2018, March 20). Jan Hus. Retrieved May 3, 2019, from http://www.newworldencyclopedia.org/entry/Jan_Hus

Editors, N. W. (2018, March 20). Jan Hus. Retrieved May 3, 2019, from https://www.newworldencyclopedia.org/entry/Jan_Hus

Editors, P. M. (2009). The Decree of Kutná Hora. Retrieved May 3, 2019, from http://www.digital-guide.cz/en/realie/education-1/the-decree-of-kutna-hora/

Editors, P. W. (2015, July 6). Today in history: Jan Hus burned at the stake 600 years ago. Retrieved May 3, 2019, from https://www.peoplesworld.org/article/today-in-history-jan-hus-burned-at-the-stake-600-years-ago/

Editors, R. P. (2006). Eucharistic Miracle of Wilsnack. Retrieved May 3, 2019, from http://www.therealpresence.org/eucharst/mir/english_pdf/Wilsnack.pdf

Editors, R. F. (2016, November 22). Jan Hus. Retrieved May 3, 2019, from http://www.religionfacts.com/jan-hus

Editors, R. (2019, January 4). Boy bishop. Retrieved May 3, 2019, from https://www.revolvy.com/page/Boy-bishop

Editors, S. P. (2015). John Wycliffe: Against Indulgences and Penance. Retrieved May 3, 2019, from http://www.scrollpublishing.com/store/Wycliffe-Indulgences.html

Editors, T. (2018). John Huss. Retrieved May 3, 2019, from https://www.theopedia.com/john-huss

Editors, Y. D. (2015). Jan Hus Facts. Retrieved May 3, 2019, from https://biography.yourdictionary.com/jan-hus

Fairchild, M. (2018, August 9). Biography of Jan Hus, Religious Reformer and Martyr. Retrieved May 3, 2019, from https://www.learnreligions.com/jan-hus-biography-4172106

Flatley, M. (2018, November 30). Regarding the crisis in our Church. Retrieved May 3, 2019, from http://catholicmissourianonline.com/stories/regarding-the-crisis-in-our-church,1327

Foxe, J. (1830). Fox's Book of Martyrs; Or, The Acts and Monuments of the Christian Church. J.J. Woodward.

Fudge, T. A. (2010). JAN HUS: Religious Reform and Social Revolution in Bohemia. Retrieved May 3, 2019, from https://www.academia.edu/38348519/Thomas_A._Fudge_-_Jan_Hus_Religious_Reform

Fudge, T. A. (2015). To Build a Fire. Retrieved May 3, 2019, from https://www.christianitytoday.com/history/issues/issue-68/to-build-fire.html

Fudge, T. A. (2015). Želivský's Head: Memory and New Martyrs Among the Hussites. Retrieved May 3, 2019, from http://www.brrp.org/proceedings/brrp6/fudge.pdf

Hayes-Healy, S. (n.d.). Medieval Paradigms: Essays in Honor of Jeremy DuQuesnay Adams, Volume 2. Springer.

Janik, V. K. (1998). Fools and Jesters in Literature, Art, and History: A Bio-bibliographical Sourcebook. Greenwood Publishing Group.

Jun, D. (2015, June 7). IN SEARCH OF JAN HUS. Retrieved May 3, 2019, from https://www.radio.cz/en/section/special/in-search-of-jan-hus

Kuhns, O., & Dickie, R. (2017). Jan Hus: Reformation in Bohemia. Lulu.com.

Laskow, S. (2017, December 29). The New Year's Feast That Transformed Fools Into Popes and Kings. Retrieved May 3, 2019, from https://www.atlasobscura.com/articles/feast-of-fools-medieval-tradition

Liardon, R. (2016). God's Generals The Martyrs. Whitaker House.

Nash, T. (2012, September 26). Life of Peasants in Medieval Times. Retrieved May 3, 2019, from http://www.thefinertimes.com/Ancient-History/the-harsh-life-of-peasants-in-medieval-times.html

O'Reggio, T. (2017). John Huss and the Origins of the Protestant Reformation. Retrieved May 3, 2019, from https://digitalcommons.andrews.edu/cgi/viewcontent.cgi?article=1579&context=jats

Pavlicek, O. (2015). The Chronology of the Life and Work of Jan Hus (F. Smahel, Ed.). Retrieved May 3, 2019, from https://www.academia.edu/37268639/The_Chronology_of_the_Life_and_Work_of_Jan_Hus

Pavlicek, O., & Šmahel, S. (2015). A Companion to Jan Hus. BRILL.

Pavlicek, O. (2018). Jan Hus as a Philosopher. Retrieved May 3, 2019, from https://www.academia.edu/38146539/Jan_Hus_as_a_Philosopher

Pope, R. M. (Ed.). (1994). Jan Huss, The Letters of John Hus [1904]. Retrieved May 3, 2019, from https://oll.libertyfund.org/titles/huss-the-letters-of-john-hus

Schaff, D. S. (1852). JOHN HUSS: HIS LIFE, TEACHINGS, AND DEATH. Retrieved May 3, 2019, from https://archive.org/stream/johnhusshislife00scha/johnhusshislife00scha_djvu.txt

Free Books by Charles River Editors

We have brand new titles available for free most days of the week. To see which of our titles are currently free, click on this link.

Discounted Books by Charles River Editors

We have titles at a discount price of just 99 cents everyday. To see which of our titles are currently 99 cents, click on this link.